Pierre Loti

Titles in the series Critical Lives present the work of leading cultural figures of the modern period. Each book explores the life of the artist, writer, philosopher or architect in question and relates it to their major works.

In the same series

Pierre Loti

Richard M. Berrong

REAKTION BOOKS

Published by Reaktion Books Ltd
Unit 32, Waterside
44–48 Wharf Road
London N1 7UX, UK

www.reaktionbooks.co.uk

First published 2018
Copyright © Richard M. Berrong 2018

Printed and bound in Great Britain by Bell & Bain, Glasgow

A catalogue record for this book is available from the British Library

ISBN 978 1 78023 995 8

Contents

Note on Texts and Abbreviations

French titles are used on first mention of a work, with an English translation in brackets; thereafter, the English translation only is given. Quotations from Loti's literary works have been referenced by chapter number, following convention in Loti scholarship. References for quotations from Loti's works are made using the following abbreviations:

Adam	Pierre Loti, *Lettres de Pierre Loti à Madame Juliette Adam (1880–1922)* (Paris, 1924)
Child	*The Story of a Child*
Disenchanted	*The Disenchanted*
Galilee	*Galilee*
Inédite	Pierre Loti, *Correspondance inédite 1865–1904*, ed. Nadine Duvignau and N. Serban (Paris, 1929)
Journal	Pierre Loti, *Journal*, 5 vols (Paris, 2006–17), ed. Alain Quella-Villéger and Bruno Vercier
Marriage	*The Marriage of Loti*
Peking	*The Last Days of Peking*
Soldats	Pierre Loti, *Soldats bleus: Journal intime 1914–1918*, ed. Alain Quella-Villéger and Bruno Vercier (Paris, 1998)
Speech	Loti's speech upon entering the French Academy: *Discours de réception à l'Académie française* (Paris, 1892)
Youth	*First Youth*
Yves	*My Brother Yves*

Where published English translations are quoted in this book, these have been indicated. All other translations are my own.

Introduction

Who was Pierre Loti and why would he be of interest to you?

A century ago readers with an interest in literature would have laughed at that question. Elected in 1891 to the French Academy, France's highest distinction for men – and more recently women – of letters, Julien Viaud, who became famous under the pen name Pierre Loti, was admired during his lifetime both in France and out as a master of prose style whose best works appealed to a broad audience as well as those with refined tastes. In his introduction to the translation of a collection of short pieces by Viaud published in England in 1898, Henry James hailed their author as a 'remarkable genius', 'one of the joys of the time', 'the companion, beyond all others, of my own selection'.[1] Willa Cather confessed that 'she would swoon with joy if anyone saw traces of Loti in her work' and assigned his masterpiece, *Pêcheur d'Islande* (Iceland Fisherman), to her students in Pittsburgh when she taught there.[2] Joseph Conrad envied him his success and mined one of his novels, *Ramuntcho*, for important elements in *Heart of Darkness*. Marcel Proust used two other Viaud novels extensively in the first part of *À la recherche du temps perdu* (In Search of Lost Time).

Since his death in 1923, however, though he remains in print in France, Viaud's name has largely disappeared from the list of French authors known outside the country, unlike, for example, his most popular contemporary and sometime rival, Émile Zola, or the younger contemporary whose work most continues in Loti's path, Proust. It is difficult to explain this disappearance.

In part, no doubt, it was because some of his foreign publishers, especially those in England and the United States, presented him largely as a travel writer and exoticist rather than a serious novelist like Zola or Proust. They repositioned half of his dozen novels to fit that then-popular genre, retitling *Aziyadé* as *Constantinople*; *Le Mariage de Loti* (The Marriage of Loti) as *Tahiti*; *Le Roman d'un spahi* (The Story of a Spahi) as *The Sahara*; *Mon frère Yves* (My Brother Yves) as *A Tale of Brittany*; *Madame Chrysanthème* (Madame Chrysanthemum) – one of the sources for Puccini's opera *Madama Butterfly* – as *Japan*; and *Ramuntcho* as *A Tale of the Pyrenees*. The beautiful coloured plates in the illustrated editions of these English translations focused on picturesque landscapes rather than specific scenes in the narratives. This tended to situate his works as light reading rather than crafted art.

Part of the problem has also been, I suspect, that some of Viaud's novels no longer work well as popular fiction and never found the more restricted audience to which they are likely to appeal, the sort of reader who enjoys works like Proust's mammoth reflection on love and art, *In Search of Lost Time*. Like Proust, Viaud knew that he was not meant to be a crafter of carefully wrought plots in the style of Balzac, Flaubert, Zola or most popular fiction.

Proust conveyed his ideas about love, memory and art in one long narrative that he developed for almost two decades. To make such a unified, long-term effort seems never to have occurred to Viaud, though he often used the same protagonist and perceived his body of work as having a similar coherence: he advised potential readers as early as 1891 from the very public podium of the French Academy that he believed the works of significant fiction writers were tied together by 'the sort of unity without which they can be neither great nor long-lasting'.[3] Had he conceptualized his literary endeavours as one sustained opus the way Proust did, he might have found a more long-lasting readership abroad as well as at home, one willing to accord his best work the serious reading that, as I will show, it merits and rewards. Even as they stand, readers will enjoy a richer experience of several of them by approaching them as fragments of a similar large, reflective exploration of the potential role of art in our lives.

Viaud conceived of his writing in terms of painting, and particularly in terms of the sort of Impressionism that Monet was developing at the time. As a result, some of his works can be read as Impressionist paintings and discussions of Impressionism. Several of his contemporaries understood that. Shortly after Viaud's death in 1923 and that of Monet in 1926, André Suarès, one of the influential founders of *La Nouvelle Revue française*, went so far as to proclaim that 'far more than Sisley, Claude Monet or the Goncourt brothers, Loti was the great Impressionist.'[4] That position may be extreme, but in 2007 French historian Franck Ferrand was still willing to assert that 'Pierre Loti [is] the only truly impressionist writer of French literature.'[5]

Another element of Viaud's opus that makes it of interest today is that he was among the first Western novelists to devote sustained sympathetic attention to the issue of male same-sex attraction. (If I use that awkward phrase rather than 'homosexuality' or any of the terms that have been developed in LGBT Studies over the last few decades, it is because they all come with much-debated denotations and connotations that do not apply to most of Viaud's work.) The author's own sexuality has been argued in private and public texts since he first became a celebrity. As we shall see, he had loving, long-term relationships with several men through most of his adult life. Over a hundred years later there is still no proof that he had sex with any of them – but for whom is that still the criterion for being homosexual? – and of course no proof that he did not, just as such negative proof has never existed for any man. More interesting is that, in an era when homosexual activity was for perhaps the first time front-page news, with the trials of Oscar Wilde in England (1895) and the Eulenburg Affair in Germany (1907–9), Viaud wrote several works that deal more or less openly with men attracted to other men and the persecution they sometimes suffered because of it. Oscar Wilde's contemporaneous *The Picture of Dorian Gray* (1890–91) is often cited as the first modern gay novel, but as Eve Kosofsky Sedgwick has remarked, 'Reading *Dorian Gray* from our twentieth-century vantage point where the name Oscar Wilde virtually *means* "homosexuality", it is worth reemphasizing how thoroughly the elements of even this novel can be read doubly or equivocally.'[6] It should be interesting to some readers to see how one of the first Western novelists to deal with these issues did so repeatedly and successfully before a general audience.

The interest of a Viaud biography does not lie solely in the discovery of some fascinating literary works, however. He had a complex and intriguing life, both in fact and as he presented it to a public eager to learn about the celebrities of its day. One of the other similarities between Viaud and Wilde was that they both made conscious and concerted use of that public's fascination with celebrities and the publications created to profit from it in order to craft often fictionalized public personas. The legendary life Viaud created for himself was arguably more exciting than Wilde's construction.[7] Though he was basically a shy individual who avoided the Parisian literary and artistic circles of his day, Viaud nevertheless came to know well several of the other celebrities of the time, among them Sarah Bernhardt, Queen Elisabeth of Romania, and the first American-born Princess of Monaco, great-great-grandmother of the reigning prince, Albert ii. Despite the catty remarks of some of his detractors, these celebrities appealed to Viaud foremost because they shared his passion for and knowledge of the arts.

Viaud served as an officer in the French navy for much of his adult life and travelled the world, both while on duty and on his own. He therefore observed the French incursion into Indochina and the Western interventions in the Ottoman Empire and China during the Boxer Rebellion. He had extended tours of duty in French Polynesia (before Robert Louis Stevenson arrived), Japan, western Africa and especially Constantinople (now Istanbul), which he visited six times. In almost all these cases he lived with the people rather than in European-catering lodging, trying, to varying degrees, to integrate himself into the local cultures. Back in France he did the same thing when stationed in the Breton and Basque regions, at a time when they were far more different from French urban culture than they are today. This biography therefore takes its readers through much of the late nineteenth- and early twentieth-century world.

All of this makes the discovery, or rediscovery, of Julien Viaud – and Pierre Loti – well worth perusing the pages that follow.

1

The Idyllic Years (1850–65)

Viaud was born on 14 January 1850, in the western French city of Rochefort, the third and very much youngest child of a Protestant family. In nineteenth-century Rochefort Protestants were a small minority. The majority of the 20,000 or so inhabitants were Catholics descended from military men settled there in the seventeenth century by Louis XIV to fight the Protestants in nearby La Rochelle. Viaud's relatives must have been fairly open-minded on this issue. His mother, Nadine Texier, was raised in a Protestant family whose ancestors experienced persecution at the time of the Revocation of the Edict of Nantes in 1685. She had nevertheless moved to the city with her mother and sister from the more Huguenot Ile d'Oléron in the 1830s. There she married a Catholic, Jean-Théodore Viaud, though she convinced him to convert so that their children could be raised in the Reformed faith. Still, when Viaud mentioned his Protestant ancestors in his works, he almost invariably evoked their persecution, which suggests that he was aware from childhood of being part of a minority that had been persecuted for its refusal to conform to social norms.

The way his family raised Viaud contributed to this feeling of being an outsider. Rather than send him to primary school, they had him instructed at home for all but one year by a succession of tutors. This was part of a general over-protection – 'excessive precautions' – that Viaud criticized repeatedly through the protagonist of one of his autobiographically based novels, *Le Roman d'un enfant* (The Story of a Child, 1881). Near the close that narrator skips for a moment past the chronological end of his narrative and remarks:

> I had to go through many years of hesitations, mistakes and fights; I had to climb many a Mount Calvary; I had to pay cruelly for having been raised as a sensitive, isolated little flower; through willpower, I had to recast and harden my physical being as well as my moral one. (*Child*, Ch. 81)

Granted, *The Story of a Child* is presented as a novel – the French title is, after all, *Le Roman d'un enfant*, though *roman* in French means both novel, the literary form, and an interesting but true life story: for example, *Et voilà le roman de ma vie*/And there's the story of my life (with 'story' carrying an implied 'complicated') The narrator in *The Story of a Child* is called Pierre by his friends and not Julien, but then Viaud's readers thought of him as Pierre Loti and not Julien Viaud, so that detail would not necessarily have signalled to them that the book is not reliable autobiography. The narrator repeatedly asserts that he is recounting the truth about his childhood even when, thanks to the work of Viaud's best modern French biographers, we know that he is not giving us the truth about the childhood of Viaud.

Viaud also has the narrator-protagonist of *The Story of a Child* explain that, when he entered middle school, he learned for the first time to play a public role – a character – that was not his real self:

> a certain superficial self, something I needed when dealing with the other boys, was already coming into being like a thin envelope, and [I] started to learn how to keep me on basically good terms with all the others, while the real myself, hidden in my depths, continued to be completely inaccessible to them. (*Child*, Ch. 75)

As we will see, that is a skill Viaud took up again during his first sojourn in Constantinople and continued to develop for the rest of his life. It was the origin of his alter-ego(s), Pierre Loti.

Despite the occasional complaints he made in middle-age, Julien Viaud seems to have had a comfortable and interesting, if occasionally lonely, childhood and early adolescence. His sister Marie was nineteen when he was born, his brother Gustave fourteen. As a result, by the time Julien was old enough to play, his siblings were both adults, though they both appear to have doted on him, as did the rest of the extended family. They all lived together in the maternal grandmother's house on what was then the rue de Chanzy (and now rue Pierre Loti) in central Rochefort. That household included Viaud's paternal and maternal grandmothers and his mother's maiden sister Clarisse. A lot of older women, as Viaud remarked more than once. (His maternal grandmother was Catholic, at least moderately senile by the time Julien came to know her, and the first of the group to die, when Julien was nine.) Within the limits of his father's city-hall salary, therefore, the boy had a pampered middle-class childhood. At one point in *The Story of a Child*, Viaud has his narrator confide to his readers that 'I usually lived with the carefree gaiety of all children' (*Child*, Ch. 12).

His brother and sister each gave him a start along one of the major routes in his adult life. In 1858 Gustave joined the navy as a surgeon and set sail for Tahiti. From there he wrote home about life at the court of the remarkable monarch, Queen Pomare IV, who ruled from 1827 until her death fifty years later. Between his rare letters and the stories and souvenirs he brought back during his one visit home in 1862, Gustave inflamed his younger brother's imagination with a desire to see the exotic parts of the world, the ones with colour – unlike whitewashed, parallel and perpendicular Rochefort. That supposedly translated first into plans to become a missionary, but eventually led Julien to decide on a career in the

Exterior of Pierre Loti's home in Rochefort.

Marie Viaud, portrait of her brother Gustave Viaud.

navy, a decision he kept secret from his parents because he knew he would have a hard time convincing them to let him follow in his brother's footsteps. *The Story of a Child* includes a scene where the older brother, home on leave, departs Rochefort to return to his service in the Pacific:

Marie Viaud, *Self-portrait*, *c.* 1851.

When he had left, the sound of the coach that was carrying him away still in our ears, my mother turned to me with a look that touched my very deepest recesses; then she drew me to her, saying, in a tone of complete confidence: 'Thank God, at least we will hold on to you!' (*Child*, Ch. 74)

His sister Marie gave Viaud other aspirations. From her youth, their father had encouraged her interest in painting, perhaps, as Alain Quella-Villéger suggests, because he regretted having had to abandon his own artistic hopes.[1] Shortly after her younger brother was born she had won scholarships from the town council to further her art studies in Paris. There she worked in the studio of Léon Cogniet, a respected Academic painter. She studied miniature painting, as was traditional for women of the era, but also painting on canvas in oils, normally the domain of men. When she returned to Rochefort for good, Jean-Théodore transformed a bedroom in their house into a studio for her, which Quella-Villéger views as an indication of how seriously both father and daughter took her aspirations to be a professional artist.[2] Marie gave the young Julien the idea that he, too, could be a professional artist. Though Cogniet probably taught a traditional approach to painting, one of Marie's letters shows that she conveyed to her younger sibling modern ideas on the subject. When she saw beauty in nature, she wrote:

> I keep looking at it, I covet it, I would like to carry it away with me . . . so that I could let someone know about it, someone who is not just one person but many people at the same time. I would like the entire world to see what I see with the same eyes, to taste it as I taste it.[3]

Thirty-four years later, during a painting trip to the Breton island Belle-Île-en-Mer, Monet would express similar goals to his then companion, later wife, Alice Hoschedé:

> I'm full of joy, but this damn ocean is terribly difficult to convey. I would like to bring back with me all of its aspects; it is so beautiful, so different. And then, I feel it as I paint it. I want to make you enjoy it, make you see what I see.[4]

Viaud also started to write as a child, sometimes supplementing his verbal efforts with visual ones. The narrator of *The Story of a Child* relates how, at the age of eight, Pierre and his friend Lucette left absurd and incoherent letters in the street so that they could enjoy the reactions of those who stopped to read them. These notes were written 'with drawings interspersed in the text as support' (*Child*, Ch. 28). The narrator concludes that chapter by asserting that 'it seems to me that I've always known how to convey the little fantasies of my imagination on paper fairly accurately with pencils or paintbrushes', emphasizing that the two arts had a close connection for him, as they would for Viaud throughout his life.

The Story of a Child also mentions the start of another interest, one for which there is no documentary evidence, though Viaud does repeat the mention in other fictional works. Even at the age of ten he experienced

> a sort of uneasy curiosity about the [area of Rochefort near the harbour] . . . to which I was never taken. Old streets perceived from a distance, empty during the day, but where, from time immemorial, sailors carried on at night during their holidays, sometimes sending the sound of their songs even as far as our house. What was going on down there? What was that brutal gaiety that we heard translated into shouts? What did they do for entertainment, those men who had returned from the sea and distant lands where the sun burns down? What was their rougher, simpler, freer life like? . . . Already the seed of an uneasiness, of an aspiration towards something different and unknown was planted in my little head . . . For a barely appreciable instant I felt deprived of the sap of life and a prisoner. (*Child*, Ch. 23)

This passage speaks to Pierre's interest in exotic lands and his feeling that his parents were being over-protective. But there is also an *uneasy* curiosity about the sailors' *brutal* gaiety, their *rougher* life, how they entertained themselves. Deprived of that knowledge, Pierre recalls that he felt *étiolé*, a French adjective used to describe plants that have been deprived of the sap that gives them basic nourishment. This is not just curiosity about new and exciting lands, therefore; this is a feeling of being deprived of something natural to him that he needs to live: something rougher, simpler, but freer.

2

Times of Crisis, Times of Decision (1865–6)

Rather than Jean-Théodore, Gustave seems to have been the chief male figure in a youth that was otherwise filled with women. Gustave's rare letters from Tahiti contained not only tales of the exotic island but advice on 'masculine' professions that Julien should consider for his future, such as engineering. During the leave he spent in Rochefort in late 1862, Gustave sought to rectify the imbalance. As Viaud later had his narrator recall in *The Story of a Child*,

> though he had barely arrived among us, [my older brother] found himself in a situation to judge [my upbringing] better. Perhaps he understood that I was experiencing a real intellectual overload as far as the arts went; that Chopin and my little theatre productions with dolls, staged with the help of a female friend, were equally dangerous for me; that I was becoming excessively refined . . . and that almost all my games involved fantasies and dreaming. So one day to my great joy he decreed that I needed to take horseback riding lessons. (*Child*, Ch. 74)

In 1919 Viaud published an autobiographically based work, *Prime Jeunesse* (First Youth), that picked up where *The Story of a Child* had left off. The narrator of that work, who bore the more autobiographical name of 'J.' rather than Pierre, declare more bluntly that the older brother insisted on equitation lessons

'out of fear that I was being raised too much like a little girl'
(*Youth*, Ch. 13).

Then, on 12 April 1865, the family received a letter announcing
that Gustave was dead. After his return from Rochefort, he had
been assigned to a military hospital in French Indochina. There,
while treating wounded French soldiers, he himself had fallen ill.
When treatment failed to cure him, he was put aboard the steamer
Alphée, bound for France. On 10 March, as it crossed the Indian
Ocean south of what is now Sri Lanka, Gustave died.

Less than a year later a second catastrophe hit. Jean-Théodore
was accused of embezzling 14,000 francs from the municipal
coffers and was dismissed from his job and even, eventually, put
in jail for several days. For a proper middle-class family in a fairly
small nineteenth-century city this was socially devastating.

It was also devastating financially. Jean-Théodore pleaded
innocent and two years later was acquitted. But he was without
his job and, worse yet, had to repay the 14,000 missing francs,
five times his annual salary. The Viauds had already been living
at the upper edge of their means, in part because they had been
able to reside with Nadine Viaud's mother in her middle-class
house. Now that Jean-Théodore's salary was gone, ends could no
longer be made to meet. The family endured the humiliation of
renting out the ground floor of their home and squeezing into
what was left upstairs. Julien experienced that humiliation
deeply and devoted the next several years to extricating his
family from it.

The family's plan had been to send him to the Polytechnic
School in Paris to study engineering, in accord with Gustave's
suggestion. That was a three-year programme, however, and
financing such studies was no longer within the family's means.
Viaud saw his opportunity and proposed entering the navy
through officers' training school, which was state funded and
demanded less time before one started earning a salary.

Whether or not Viaud was aware of it at the time, this reversal of his aspirations was again, at least indirectly, his older brother's doing. Though the family maintained and may well have believed in Jean-Théodore's innocence, we now know that he did in fact embezzle those funds, evidently to cover his older son's gambling debts. So, just as Gustave's death in the navy almost deprived Julien of a chance to pursue the adventures of his dreams, so Gustave's financial imprudence and his father's desperation to hide it re-enabled him.

In *First Youth* Viaud also recounted an event for which there is no corroborating documentation, one that some of his biographers have greeted with scepticism. The 69-year-old Viaud informed his reading public that during the summer of 1866, after his father had been accused of embezzlement but before young J. left for Paris to prepare for the naval officers' training school entrance exam, he was introduced to sex by a young gypsy. Viaud had never alluded to such an event in any of the often very personal autobiographical writings he had published over the four previous decades. Gypsies depicted as over-sexed seducers of young men and women constituted a nineteenth-century European literary cliché.[1] Whether or not it is authentic, however, this episode merits examination as an example of how Julien Viaud went about constructing his complex alter-ego Pierre Loti.

From the beginning, the narrator couches the episode as a passage from boyhood to manhood: he explains that it began one warm summer evening when his sixteen-year-old self joined a group of his brother-in-law's adult male friends, who were speaking of a beautiful gypsy woman 'among men' (*Youth*, Chs. 25–30). Shortly thereafter the gypsy appears. She is driven away by a servant, though not before she exchanges apparently inviting glances with young J. His much older self recalls that her dark skin was the 'colour of old Etrurian terracottas', which links her to Viaud's first major literary success, the novel *The Marriage of*

Loti (1880), in which Rarahu, the Tahitian girl with whom the protagonist, English sailor Harry Grant (Loti), falls in love, is also described as having skin resembling 'the light-coloured terracottas of old Etruria' (*Marriage*, Ch. 5). Like Rarahu, this young gypsy is also presented as resembling classical art: her chest evokes that of a statue.

The young gypsy seems to offer this provincial young Protestant knowledge of all the secrets of sex that had been hidden from him by his nineteenth-century middle-class upbringing:

> What was most fascinating about her were her eyes, full of depth and the night, – behind which, who knows, there was perhaps nothing, but where you would have said that all the sensual mysticism of India was hiding. (*Youth*, Ch. 25)

In subsequent days J. visits her in the Roche Corbon grotto near the gypsy camp outside Saint-Porchaire in southwestern France and they have sex.[2]

Did this actually happen to the sixteen-year-old Julien Viaud? In a passage in his diary for 20 August 1893, 26 years before he penned *First Youth*, Viaud stated that he had only been in the Roche Courbon grotto once before, when he was around fifteen, with a male relative around his own age, André You. Furthermore, the episode in *First Youth* is modelled on the meeting with a young fisherman of Gaud Mével, the female protagonist of Viaud's most popular novel, *Iceland Fisherman* (1886), who is herself modelled on Viaud. All this suggests that Viaud did not meet a gypsy in that grotto at that age, though perhaps he had some sort of sexual experience with his young male relative.

What is clear, however, is that the 69-year-old Viaud developed this incident to further shape his readers' image(s) of the adventurous life of Pierre Loti. At that point in his life Viaud clearly wanted his readers to imagine that he had had a confusing and ambiguous initiation into the mysteries of sex for which his younger self was not altogether, if at all, responsible. For Viaud's faithful readers the real gender and identity of the obviously cliché-ridden gypsy would have *depended on how well they remembered some of his previous work*. At least some readers familiar with that previous work would have recollected the scenes in *Iceland Fisherman*, perhaps encouraged to do so by the suggestion Viaud had made to virtually all of France from the podium of the French Academy that there was underlying his corpus 'the sort of unity without which there can be neither great nor long-lasting works' (*Speech*, 61). Expecting at least some of his readers to make that sort of memory effort would have been natural in a work that is devoted to recollection and the workings of memory.

On 9 October 1866, while his father was in jail, Julien Viaud boarded the train for Paris.

3

Paris in the 1860s

At sixteen, never having experienced a city larger than provincial Rochefort Julien Viaud found himself in Paris, the largest city in continental Europe. It was also the centre of the world of art. The Louvre and Luxembourg Palace art museums figure regularly in the letters he sent to Marie. In the first one he was dismissive of the copy work he saw students doing there, a traditional part of art studies, and announced that he could and would do better – although he also decided that he needed to take formal instruction in painting, as his sister had done before him.

Before he left Rochefort he had asked Marie's advice on which paintings to copy. She evidently recommended those by the old Italian masters, which were held by the Parisian art establishment of the time as the supreme models to be emulated. Part of the scandal caused by *Le Déjeuner sur l'herbe*, which had been rejected by the Paris Salon three years before Viaud's arrival, was that Manet had in fact modelled it on a painting by Raphael, the most revered of the Italian masters, but in ways that could not be brooked by the Salon judges. As part of their artistic revolution, the Impressionists would reject modelling painting on other artworks rather than nature itself. When Viaud, shortly after the conclusion of his Paris studies a year later, takes up painting in Brittany, he will assure his sister that 'I feel I will, as you say, have enough feeling for nature to succeed if I work at it a little' (*Inédite*, 59).

Viaud found no old Italian master landscapes in the Louvre. He was, however, particularly fascinated by several canvases of

Nicolaes Pieterszoon Berchem, *Italian Landscape*, 1650–83, oil on canvas.

the Dutch painter Nicolaes Pieterszoon Berchem (1620–1683), from the next generation after Rembrandt. The Dutch masters, as opposed to the Italian ones, were generally anathema to French Academic teachers of the nineteenth century, whereas Rembrandt in particular was being taken as an inspiration by several of the Impressionists, including Monet.[1] Viaud describes the Berchem landscapes as being 'all of mountains and lakes, in the mist, without trees', very different from the line-centred work of Raphael and the other great Renaissance Italian artists (*Inédite*, 15). He closed that first letter by telling his sister that he could not stop admiring the masterpieces in the Great Hall of the Louvre.

In her 2017 book on nineteenth-century French novelists who dealt with painting in their works, Anka Muhlstein provides the historical context necessary to appreciate Viaud's strong reaction:

Théodore Géricault, *The Raft of the Medusa*, *c*. 1817–19, oil on canvas.

Having easy access to great works by visiting a museum feels so obvious to us now that we rarely think of the cultural revolution brought about by the advent of modern museums [in the nineteenth century]. And yet what a sea change in behavior this opportunity afforded. Before the Revolution only birthright or unusual personal success opened the door to masterpieces held in palaces and mansions, or to galleries of fine paintings acquired by wealthy Parisian collectors . . . Wandering at will and at one's own speed around the Louvre's Grande Galerie was, therefore, a priceless experience – both literally, because admittance was free, and metaphorically.[2]

Viaud sent Marie another letter, on a Monday, unable to wait until Saturday, his weekly epistle-writing day, so that he could share with her his reactions to his second visit to the Louvre. This time he admired Théodore Géricault's romantic *Raft of the Medusa* (*c*. 1817–19)

Anne-Louis Girodet de Roucy-Trioson, *The Entombment of Atala*, 1808, oil on canvas.

and Anne-Louis Girodet's more classical *Entombment of Atala* (1808), as well as, once again, the Berchems. He kept repeating that he was overwhelmed: *ébloui, ébahi*. 'I want to go to the Louvre every day I have free' (*Inédite*, 19). In short, young Viaud took art and his practice of it very seriously and was extremely excited about it.

By 1866 art in Paris was not restricted to the great public museums and the Salon, an annual or bi-annual government-sponsored art show – success at which could launch a career. Particularly after the scandal of the 1863 Salon, which had rejected a record number of works in addition to Manet's *Déjeuner sur l'herbe*, artists, mostly the young and innovative, sought other venues for their work. A growing number of art lovers began to accept that the Paris art establishment was not, after all, the supreme arbiter of what constituted greatness, though it was still likely to be found in Paris. As the city in general and the art world in particular geared up for the Universal Exhibition that would open in April 1867, at which Napoleon III intended to demonstrate to the world France's supremacy in the arts as in other fields, various private galleries displayed the works of some of these revolutionary painters. Near the end of his stay in the capital, on 6 May 1867, Viaud wrote to his sister: 'I saw the Exhibition Thursday. I'd really like to tell you about it, but I don't have the time', suggesting that he had a lot to say (*Inédite*, 47). Fifty-two years later, however, in *First Youth*, Viaud mentioned the exhibition only for its 'loud, common noise', which he set in contrast to the quiet of the hall where he took the officers' school entrance exam (*Youth*, Ch. 47). In that much later text he assures his readers that 'Paris neither surprised me nor filled me with wonder.' Why he chose to deny his youthful excitement it is hard to say.

One other event with long-term consequences happened while Viaud was in Paris. Describing how lonely and unhappy he was there, at least from his 1919 perspective, the narrator of *First Youth* explains that

> in order to escape from the moroseness of the present and plunge even more into my beloved past – which was still recent – I undertook to write something like my memoirs. This new manuscript, inaugurated on a rainy Sunday in November [1866], no longer took the form of an endless roll of paper with a cabbalistic appearance covered only with cryptographs, like my first attempt at the diary genre in the past. No, this was a simply bound little notebook, but still with a mysterious appearance because, to make it easy to hide, it was on very thin onionskin paper covered with flyspecks that were barely legible because they were so fine. I would have died of embarrassment if anyone had cast his eyes on it. Such was the beginning of this diary of my life, which today, alas, comprises more than two hundred volumes . . . Still, I almost never recorded what happened during my days, which

didn't much interest me, but only things from the past, to
keep them from escaping from me altogether. (*Youth*, Ch. 38)

The novels, travelogues and autobiographical fictions that he
derived from it throughout his life almost all have in common this
effort to prevent sensations 'from escaping from [him] altogether'.
In fact, Viaud kept this diary faithfully from 1866 to the end of 1911,
after which he added to it sporadically. He resumed the practice
in 1914–18 during his war service, then set it aside again, that time
permanently, entering nothing further for the last five years of his
life. This diary constitutes the single most important source for the
reconstruction of his biography.

Despite any noise he may have heard from the Universal
Exhibition in the test room, on 12 July 1867, the seventeen-year-old
Julien Viaud did well enough on the naval school entrance exam to
score fortieth out of sixty. By October he was aboard the *Borda*, an
officers' training ship anchored in the harbour of Brest in western
Brittany.

4

In the Navy (1867–77)

As they would for the length of his career as a naval officer, Viaud's
obligations as a navy student left him time for art. Within a month
of his arrival in Brest he informed Marie that he was sketching
views seen from the porthole of his cabin on the *Borda* and had
applied for permission to have a box of oils because 'the sea is still
too difficult for me. It seems to me that I would have more success
with oils' (*Inédite*, 59). Already he was aware of the challenges
posed by painting the North Atlantic, challenges he would meet
in an Impressionist fashion two decades later in his best novel,
Iceland Fisherman. His reaction to the Breton countryside while on
shore leave was that he desperately wanted to paint it as well: 'This
Brittany is decidedly a charming country; I never felt such a rage to
paint' (*Inédite*, 66). His artwork eventually attracted the attention
and admiration of his commanding officers.

Viaud continued to explore Brittany during his time on the
Borda. In his diary entry for 20 August 1868 he described the
countryside around the town of Port-Louis:

> We found a vague resemblance to the swampy undergrowth
> of the Lias [Early Jurassic] period . . . Sea pines did a good
> job of imitating the gigantic calamites found in primitive
> forests. The heat was heavy. The foggy, leaden sky recalled
> the thick atmosphere of the ancient world. (*Journal 1*, 46)

Viaud had been interested in the prehistoric world as a child and had owned illustrated books showing reconstructions of prehistoric landscapes just as children do today. What is significant here is that, as he would do almost two decades later in his two Breton-set novels, already in 1868 Viaud was seeing rural Brittany as still manifesting its prehistoric past.

The passage just quoted from Viaud's diary no longer figures in the manuscript as we have it today; the editors of the critical edition reproduced it from a journal article published in 1959 whose author had access to the diary manuscript then. This is therefore a good time to explain the state in which we have the diary today and its reliability, since from now on it will be the most important, if problematic, source for this biography.

As Alain Quella-Villéger and Bruno Vercier explain in the Introduction to their critical edition of the diary, we still have most of the original notebooks in which Viaud recorded his feelings and actions, but pages and even entire notebooks are missing. To fill those gaps, the editors have made use, with all necessary disclaimers, of various published collections of excerpts, especially the edition of the early part of the diary brought out near the end of his life by Viaud himself and his legitimate son, Samuel.[1] But, as we can see if we compare that early edition with pages of the diary manuscript that do survive, much was radically rewritten. Samuel Viaud even omitted some passages and created others on his own from scratch.

Moreover, the diary manuscript pages that do survive are not necessarily what Viaud originally wrote. He, and then Samuel, and then Samuel's widow, all took turns crossing out passages and rewriting others with an eye to the Loti legacy as they understood it.

Even the unaltered original is sometimes only a 'real' diary to a certain extent. After deriving four novels from its pages, Viaud realized that he would continue to mine it for future texts and started to write it, at least sometimes, not as spontaneous jottings but as an artistically conscious first draft for future literary works. As he explained to a journalist from one of the large Parisian newspapers, *Le Figaro*, in 1887,

> In the past, [when I wrote my diary] I was happy just taking notes for myself, having no idea that they would ever be published. . . . Today I continue to take notes but it is no longer with the candour of the past, I admit it; it's with an awareness that I will publish them, that I will draw books out of them. (*Journal I*, 17)

And then, of course, how many of us really write the whole truth and nothing but the truth in our diaries, even when we have no intention of publishing them? In short, while it is very useful for the biographer, Viaud's diary as we have it today is not a completely reliable text.

Once he started looking at contemporary Bretons as individuals still connected to prehistory, they became, for Viaud, an important exception to the late nineteenth-century European belief that modern Western man was undergoing physical and moral degeneration. As Robert A. Nye has shown, various French scientists spent the second half of the century promulgating the idea that

> mankind had degenerated from a pristine Adamite stock through the slow accumulation of inherited defects. These defects had taken root in populations that were exposed to environmental pathogens, suffered poor nourishment, or were addicted to vice: they ramified in complexity and seriousness until sterility terminated a breeding line.[2]

France's declining birthrate and a change to the feminine in the ratio of male to female births played into this theory of national degeneration, convincing some French scientists and politicians that 'in France degeneration was a *national* syndrome producing a *national* disease.'[3]

At the same time, nineteenth-century republican French historians were reworking the traditional view of the origin of the French people to argue that Charlemagne and the Franks, who founded many of France's noble lineages, had been outsiders: Germans. 'Real' Frenchmen, the people, those historians argued, were descended from the pre-Frankish Celts.[4] Statues of the most famous of those Celts, Julius Caesar's long-ignored opponent Vercingetorix, started appearing across France.[5] Some of these same republican historians argued that the part of France whose inhabitants were the closest to those Celts, the least corrupted by the Romans and the various tribes who had invaded the region since, was Brittany. When Viaud set two of his most popular novels, *My Brother Yves* (1883) and *Iceland Fisherman* (1886), in Brittany, he

Frédéric-Auguste Bartholdi, *Vercingetorix*, 1903, Clermont-Ferrand.

Pierre Loti, *Limoise 12 August 1869 8:00 in the morning,* 1869.

presented their Breton characters, especially the male protagonists, as individuals with direct links to prehistoric men and nature, endowing them with a force, primarily physical but also moral, that made them superior to products of nineteenth-century French urban civilization.

Marie continued to provide him with artistic counsel. In late 1869 or early 1870, she advised her brother about his writing in a way that, once again, recalls the work of Monet: 'Write down your impressions pell-mell,' she told him; 'jot down what makes you enthusiastic . . . you'll be delighted with it later, I assure you.'[6]

Maurice E. Chernowitz has defined Monet's Impressionist techniques in much the same way:

> one of the most vital characteristics of pictorial Impressionism . . . is the emphasis on aconceptual sensation . . . this instantaneous first impression involves the reaction which is experienced before the intellect has had time to intervene and interpret things in conventional, rational, causal terms.[7]

Joseph Bernard with Loti.

We can see Viaud's efforts to follow his sister's counsel in some
of the drawings he made during a furlough spent in Rochefort. For
example, *Limoise 12 August 1869 8:00 in the morning* demonstrates
a desire to capture a quick initial impression as it appeared for just
a moment in a particular light.[8]

At the end of their second year of studies, Viaud's class was sent
on an extensive voyage aboard the *Jean-Bart*, one that introduced
him to many ports of call and different cultures. While he was at
sea Viaud received news that his father had died, leaving the family
deep in debt and Viaud with the feeling that he was responsible for
helping them. In late summer 1870 the *Jean-Bart* returned to France
and Viaud, his studies complete, was commissioned a midshipman
first class. On 15 March 1871, he was sent out on the *Flore* for his first
voyage to the other side of the world.

With Viaud was another member of his *Borda* class, Joseph Bernard, whom for the next several years Viaud would depict as his intimate friend, his 'brother'; indeed Bernard was the first in a line of tall, handsome, athletic men whom Viaud would choose to occupy that position in his life. Already, in a letter of 23 April 1870, Viaud had exclaimed to Marie: 'If you knew how much I love him and how much he is worthy of it' (*Inédite*, 99). Once they were sailing around the globe together, Viaud's feelings for Bernard became downright domestic. From Valparaiso, Chile, he wrote to Marie that when they got to Tahiti 'our intention is to rent a cottage there in order to establish our *home* for two.' Viaud used the English word *home*, 'notre *home* à deux', a construction one uses in French to speak of a couple's romantic love-nest (*Inédite*, 120). Marie was evidently apprehensive about what this language, the endless 'we's and 'our's, implied. Viaud ended a subsequent letter to her with the assurance that 'we are not at all in love, as you might suppose' (*Inédite*, 125). Whatever the nature of their relationship, Bernard had become sufficiently close to his 'brother' that he helped him finance the purchase of the Rochefort house from Viaud's mother Nadine so that she would not have to sell it to strangers to pay off her recently deceased husband's debts.[9]

One of the tasks assigned the *Flore* was to study the great stone heads on Easter Island and bring one back. (The one they transported would be set up in the Jardin des Plantes, not far from where Viaud had lived when he studied in Paris. It is now in the Musée de l'Homme at the other end of the city.) Thanks to the intervention of Nelly Lieutier, a Paris relative by his sister Marie's marriage to Albert Bon who had contacts in the publishing world, several of Viaud's drawings of these stone heads and other aspects of the island were published later that year in *L'Illustration*, an illustrated magazine with a wide circulation. It was the first time Viaud had either his art or his prose published, much less in such an important venue, and it reinforced his intent to pursue one or the other of those fields as a profession once he completed his time with the navy – at that point, he did not yet see himself as a career naval officer.

He did, however, feel a certain artistic inadequacy that would trouble him throughout his life. In his diary Viaud wrote:

> The drawing that I did of [the stone head] is powerless
> to convey the fantastic aspect of the craters, with their
> strong contrasts of shadow and light, standing out against
> a black sky. Neither does it convey the cries or the frenzy
> [of the locals who were watching the French carry off that
> giant part of their religious heritage]. (*Journal I*, 108)[10]

Even at this point, Viaud wanted his art to convey not just the visual aspect of his motif, but the sounds and feelings associated with it as well. As we will see, this continued to be a preoccupation even when he focused on his textual art.

Viaud already had this problem with language when he arrived in Tahiti. Speaking to his diary in a rather rhetorical fashion about an evening spent with Taüvira, a boy who might have been his brother Gustave's son by a Tahitian woman, Viaud wondered:

> Where in French can one find words that translate something
> of that Polynesian night, the desolate sounds of nature, of
> the great, sonorous woods, of that solitude in the immensity
> of that Ocean . . . of those forests filled with whistles and
> strange noises, peopled with ghosts? (*Journal I*, 146)[11]

Viaud was convinced that there were certain things specific to a culture that only the language produced by that culture could convey. His preoccupation with finding the right evocative words shows the influence of his favourite novelist, Gustave Flaubert.

Tahiti was the farthest point west for the *Flore* and its longest port of call, from late January to March of 1872, and then, after a call at San Francisco, again in June and July. Viaud had more than drawing to keep him busy. Like many of his fellow sailors, he spent time on the island discovering the beautiful flora and two-legged fauna for which it was then and is still justifiably famous. He got to know Queen Pomare IV, as his brother had before him, and spoke with her about him.

He also spent time searching for what remained of Gustave's sojourn there ten years before. The house he had occupied with a Tahitian woman, Tarahu, still stood, and Viaud was able to meet her. 'Did she have children with Gustave?', it suddenly occurred to him to ask her (*Journal I*, 118–23). 'Yes', she replied, but it was too late to get them before Viaud's departure for San Francisco. 'When I return?', he requested. Yes, she would bring him the children when he returned.

When Viaud got back to Tahiti in June, Tarahu did bring her children, including a boy named Taüvira whom she presented as Gustave's son. Viaud was thrilled to find a survivor of his brother, but eventually birth records showed that the boy must have had a different father. In 1974 Clive Wake argued that the author had not grown out of the 'homosexual hero-worship stage of his adolescence' because of his fixation on Gustave, but I don't know that anyone today would subscribe to either that explanation of male same-sex desire or that concept of human psychological development.[12]

Even though Viaud could not bring back a living continuation of his beloved brother, he did leave Tahiti with something that would define him for the rest of his life: a new name. Someone on the island, perhaps the young women in Pomare IV's court, took to calling him *Loti*. Scholars have argued since about which Tahitian word that might have been, but it doesn't really matter, since Viaud's readers have taken Viaud's word that it designates a flower.[13] When he started publishing novels, at first anonymously,

Pierre Loti, *Easter Island, 7 January, 1872, around 5:00 a.m.*, 1872.

in the years to come, their autobiographically based protagonist would bear the name Loti – as, eventually, when Viaud had to put an author's name on them, would the books themselves.

By the end of the year Viaud was back in France. His sister was still painting and their letters were still filled with talk about art. Viaud worked on some of his drawings from French Polynesia and was pleased to report to Marie that *L'Illustration* had increased what they paid to reproduce them. This money went to reduce the debt he had incurred to buy the family home. He also kept up a correspondence with Joseph Bernard, who had returned to his native Lille and to whom Viaud sent 'tender kisses' (*Journal I*, 168). They were working with Bernard's uncle to arrange an appointment for the two of them to the West African French outpost in Senegal, and succeeded. Viaud joined Bernard there in September 1873. Once in Dakar he decorated a cottage for the two of them, as he had looked forward to doing in Tahiti. By the end of the year he was also asking Marie to send him special paper for watercolours; *L'Illustration* was still publishing engravings of his work. He also became entangled in an affair with a European woman who was in Senegal with her husband.

Viaud found that he could not keep all these balls in the air indefinitely. In the first part of 1874 Joseph Bernard asked to be recalled to France, leaving Viaud in Africa asking why his 'brother' had abandoned him. Bernard left the navy before the end of the year. Viaud, back in France himself by then, recalled in his diary: 'Once upon a time we arranged our future for each other . . . and we believed we could no longer live separated from each other' (*Journal I*, 232). Joseph's radical actions did not make sense to him, but Viaud kept sending him letters, concluding one with 'if our great love as brothers has vanished, it will at least always be the sweetest memory of my life' (*Journal I*, 234).

The European woman had also left Senegal in June, taken to Switzerland by her husband. In his diary that month Viaud, addressing Bernard, wrote: 'you abandoned me, – I've lost her as well', suggesting that he saw himself linked to Bernard and the woman by the same sort of ties (*Journal 1*, 225). Once Viaud was back in Europe he went to see her in Geneva, in part because he had learned that their affair had resulted in a child. She did not want anything further to do with him.

Viaud decided to withdraw from active duty, at least for a while. In January 1875, he took a sixth-month leave and enrolled at the military academy in Joinville-le-Pont, just outside Paris. He had been a frail child. Now he decided to toughen up. For six months he undertook rigorous physical training, bringing his body under complete control. For the rest of his life he remained a physical fitness devotee, practising a wide variety of sports to keep in shape. His first encounter with the great French actress Sarah Bernhardt, with whom he became good friends for many years, evidently also occurred while he was studying in Joinville-le-Pont.

He occasionally heard from Joseph Bernard, who did not write very often but evidently did not want to break off communications altogether. In a missive of 30 April 1875, Bernard joked that he saw himself in a not too distant future bouncing Viaud's large pack of young children on his knee while 'you paint for art and business in your studio'.[14] Viaud evidently still saw and presented himself as someone who would have a career as a professional painter.

In April 1876, back on active duty at the naval port of Toulon on the French Mediterranean coast, Viaud appeared as an acrobat with the Etruscan Circus. He was sufficiently proud of the body he had built that he designed his own costume to show it off, had it made in Paris and had himself photographed in it. The next month he was aboard the *Couronne* as it set sail for Salonica (today Thessaloníki) in the Ottoman Empire to deal with a much-exaggerated case of political unrest.

Ever since the end of the Crimean War (1853–6), England and France had been manoeuvring to lessen the power of their former

Loti in circus costume, 1876.

ally the Ottoman Empire and acquire control of parts of it. On 6 May 1876, a Bulgarian Christian girl in Salonica who had converted to Islam was attacked by a Greek (Christian) group at a railway station and had her veil torn off. Muslims rushed to avenge the insult, and during the fighting that ensued the French and German consuls were killed. The western European press inflated this into a horror story of Muslims slaughtering Christians under the indifferent nose of the Ottoman Empire. That was enough justification for England and France to send warships to 'protect the Christians'.

The *Couronne* was one of the ships the French government dispatched. Napoleon III's Second Empire had fallen in 1870, so the just recently established French Third Republic was intent on showing that it had its military house in order and was still capable of playing a major role in international affairs – in other words, that it was not going to allow the British to gobble up the 'third world' by themselves. After two months in Salonica, Viaud was transferred to the aggressively named *Gladiateur*, stationed near the capital of the Ottoman Empire, Constantinople, where it stayed until March 1877.

While his country played intimidation politics with the Ottomans, Viaud took advantage of this extended stay to do what separates travellers from tourists: he left his safety zone of Western culture, the officers' quarters on the *Gladiateur* and the European part of the city, Pera, to set up a household among the Turks in the old part of Constantinople. Soon he was dressing like a Turk, adopting at least some of their daily routines, and making a serious effort to learn their language – he who felt that parts of a culture could only be expressed in the words of that culture. He claimed to have worked so hard on the language that he was able to speak and understand it after two months. We will never know how honest he was about this, but with immersion, hard work and a gift for languages a lot can be accomplished in two months. On occasion, of course, he had to report to the *Gladiateur* and do what was required of him as an officer. The rest of the time, however, which seems to have been most of it, he lived more or less as a Turk on shore. How well he brought this off and how much the locals were just flattering his ego we have no way of knowing.

As he discovered and confided to his diary, Constantinople was a place 'where one can carry on several different personalities' (*Journal I*, 325). This provided a solution to a difficult personal situation for a man who had long been interested in the theatre. Henceforth, when on his own, Viaud would do exactly as he pleased, because in Turkish Constantinople, unlike nineteenth-century middle-class provincial France, no one meddled in your personal affairs. He would work at making Loti a very liberated, pleasure-seeking guy, a development of the man who had first started to blossom, with the help of Tahitians, in Polynesia. He wrote from Constantinople:

> There is no God, there is no morality. None of the things we have been taught to respect actually exists. My unique rule of conduct is always to do what pleases me, in spite of all morality, all social conventions. – I believe in nothing and no one, I love no one and nothing. I have neither faith nor hope. (*Journal I*, 290)

Or, as he had already written from Salonica to one of his classmates from the *Borda*, Léon Baudin, 'everything that is pleasing is good to do, and you always need to spice as best you can the stew of life' (*Journal I*, 271). When the occasion called for it, he could still play the part – which would henceforth only be a part – of Julien Viaud. He had found a place where he could spend almost all his time living as the man he wanted to be, however, rather than the one imposed upon him by his birth, family and culture.

Much of that stew involved romantic affairs, of course. Some were with unidentified individuals, apparently but not necessarily all women, with whom he passed many a night. In Constantinople, he confided to his diary:

around my house stretched vast fields that overlooked Stamboul, planted with cypress and tombs, empty fields where I spent more than one night, pursuing some imprudent Greek or Armenian adventure . . . Of these beautiful creatures I have retained only the charmless memory left by the burning love of the senses; nothing more ever attached me to any of them, and they were quickly forgotten . . . (*Journal I*, 293)[15]

There was one 'creature' in particular, Hakidjé, a young woman whom he met in Salonica and then in Constantinople, with whom it seems he fell in love and with whom he carried on a difficult relationship, difficult because she was one of the wives of a wealthy but evidently not very watchful Turkish merchant.[16] In the diary as we have it now, this is a tale of secret, romantic rendezvous, stolen moments and kisses. Just the sort of thing to inflame the heart, imagination and senses of a romantic 26-year-old who, after having discovered during a few weeks on Tahiti what it had deprived him of, was trying to free himself from a moralistic Protestant upbringing in a small city that allowed few secrets.

There was also a young man, Daniel, with 'a very handsome head, – a great sweetness in his eyes, in which shone honesty and intelligence' (*Journal I*, 268). The first time Viaud met him, shortly after arriving in Salonica, Daniel was barely clothed, his feet bare, his legs bare, his shirt in tatters. They soon formed a 'brotherly intimacy', a word choice indicating that this handsome young man had become Joseph Bernard's replacement, if not successor. One night Viaud invited him to share his bed rather than sleep on the hard floor next to it, as was Daniel's custom. Daniel evidently understood this as a romantic invitation and took Viaud in his arms, kissing him. But, says the diary, Viaud pushed him away 'without anger', telling him:

No . . . that's not what I want from you, my poor Daniel.
You've misunderstood. In my country this sort of love is
condemned and forbidden. Don't do this again, or I will
have you arrested tomorrow by the police. (*Journal 1*, 275)[17]

Viaud demonstrates no moralistic outrage. Even Lesley Blanch,
who could not countenance the idea of a gay Pierre Loti, conceded
that at this moment Viaud 'does not appear to have made very
convincing efforts to discourage Samuel [Daniel]'.[18] If Viaud
condemns anything, it is the morality of his own country. When he
has to return to France a year later he will describe it as 'rule-driven
and policed' (*Journal 1*, 408).[19]

   This open-minded Viaud describes Daniel's feelings for him as
'love', which few western European writers in 1876 or some time
after that would have been willing to do.[20] As we saw earlier in
this chapter, French scientists in the second half of the nineteenth
century believed that the French 'race', especially its men, was in a
serious state of decline. After the humiliating loss of the Franco-
Prussian War in 1870, many Frenchmen, looking for exculpatory
explanations, took to arguing, among other things, that their
country had lost the war because its tolerance for homosexuality
was resulting in weak Frenchmen. If it wanted to win the next,
inevitable war with Germany, the nation needed to condemn
and eradicate this physically and morally debilitating plague.[21]
To describe Daniel's apparently homosexual embrace as love
rather than perversion, as it was being presented in French and
German medical journals of the day, was in 1876 open-minded in
the extreme.[22] Over a century later, some of the scholars who have
written on Loti have not been so open-minded, as in the case of
Irene Szyliowicz, even while she condemns Viaud for having old-
fashioned ideas about 'Oriental' women.[23]

   Despite knowing Daniel's feelings for him, though not
exploring his own for Daniel, Viaud eventually allowed the young

man to share his bed.[24] Daniel subsequently followed Viaud to Constantinople, where they shared a humble house together – with separate bedrooms – while Viaud saw Hakidjé and, on occasion, those gender-non-specific Greek and Armenian individuals in the nearby fields. When Daniel disappeared for a few days, Viaud apostrophized him in the diary as he had previously an absent Joseph Bernard:

> Come back, my dear Daniel, I love you, my friend, my brother, I feel it now. I will probably never see you again, but when I come back in the evening to my deserted house, my heart tightens because you are no longer here. (*Journal 1*, 288–9)[25]

In November, Viaud wrote to Léon Baudin saying that he loved Hakidjé 'almost, and it is for her that I have become a Turk . . . I love Daniel a great deal, and he loves me with adoration' (*Journal 1*, 304).[26] In December, he informed Marie that 'I have never loved anyone as much as [Joseph Bernard], I loved him with adoration' (*Journal 1*, 310).[27] Constantinople opened Viaud to all types of love.

Then, in March 1877, the *Gladiateur*, having sufficiently intimidated the Ottoman government, was called back to France. As it sailed away, Viaud thought about Hakidjé: 'I will still love her when I am no longer young, when it is no longer a question of the charm of physical attraction, in the mysterious future that will bring us old age and death.' He also thought about Mehmed, a handsome young Turk who had replaced Daniel in his household and his affections by the end of his stay: 'My poor little friend Mehmed, I still really loved him. His friendship was sweet and beneficial to me' (*Journal 1*, 398–9).[28]

5

A Successful Author – and Alter-ego – Is Born (1877–81)

When Viaud arrived back in France in April 1877, even his imagination may not have envisioned the radical changes in store for him.

Certainly he had hopes for his projected career as a painter. To that end, and to help pay down the debt he had incurred to buy the family home, he continued to publish drawings in the nation's widely circulated illustrated weeklies. Salon prize-winning painters supplemented their income by illustrating texts in such magazines, so the endeavour was not considered unworthy of a serious artist.

He also discovered that even in France he could 'carry on several different personalities', both some of those he had developed in Constantinople and new ones. He was still in love with Hakidjé and wanted her to leave the Turkish merchant and join him in France. He does not seem to have considered the problems this would have caused his Protestant middle-class mother or his chances for promotion as a naval officer, which he may not yet have seen as a permanent career. Nor does he seem to have thought about the situation of non-French-speaking Hakidjé herself, a young woman not accustomed to fending for herself, who in France would have been a fish out of her familiar cultural waters, completely dependent on a young man deeply in debt. He continued to send her letters through Mehmet – whom he had not forgotten either.

Since his amorous adventures in Constantinople were still on his mind, it is not surprising that he recounted them to his fellow officers at the naval base in Toulon, even reading those parts of his diary to them. These friends found the story so entertaining that they encouraged him to publish it and undertook to help him do so.

Inspired by his friends' praise, Viaud undertook a first revision of his diary entries, among other things adding an ending to the love story so that the work did not conclude with the cliché of the European man leaving the exotic young woman loved in a foreign land, never to return, a cliché that would be attributed to Viaud in years to come. In this first revision, entitled *Béhidgé*, the young naval officer, transformed into Harry Grant of Her Majesty's Navy, returns to Constantinople, finds that Béhidgé has died for love of him, and joins the Ottoman army, dying shortly thereafter in the Battle of Kars. Viaud made two copies of this revision. One, which we will call A, he sent to Nelly Lieutier, who had arranged for the publication of his drawings in *L'Illustration*. He kept the other, B, so that he could work on it with his friend and fellow naval officer C. de Polignac.

Though he already had self-assurance as a graphic artist built upon significant publications, Viaud evidently did not at this point feel secure enough as a writer to attempt the transformation of his diary into a novel completely by himself. When he was sent to the Lorient naval base in Brittany in November, he left the partially reworked manuscript B with Polignac. In January he told Lucien Jousselin, another friend and fellow officer, that he was working on a 'little novel' 'together with' Polignac, not that he had written it by himself and Polignac was just helping him polish it (*Journal I*, 420). Polignac also had connections in the publishing world and was close to getting a contract from Édouard Dentu, a major Paris publishing house.

Perhaps because he was now reliving their adventures through his developing manuscript, perhaps just because it was true, Viaud kept telling his diary at this time that he still loved Hakidjé 'with all my soul and all my heart' (*Journal I*, 417).[1]

In the end, Dentu rejected manuscript B. Polignac turned it over to their common friend Jousselin. Jousselin set about making his own revisions without consulting Viaud, who was by then on the *Tonnerre* patrolling the Breton coast.

Viaud was not out of touch, however. Nelly Lieutier had done nothing about placing manuscript A, so Viaud had her turn it over to yet another friend and fellow naval officer, Victor Lampérière. Lampérière negotiated for a lucrative serialization in the Parisian daily *L'Événement* and then sent A to Viaud, who started to revise it and renamed it *Aziyadé*. Only then did he learn that Jousselin, in addition to undertaking negotiations with Calmann-Lévy, another major Paris publishing house, had also made extensive moral and stylistic revisions to B. On 16 February 1878 Jousselin signed a contract with Calmann-Lévy.

Viaud was not happy. He started by sending Jousselin manuscript A with his revisions on it, asking him to incorporate these into Jousselin's revised manuscript B. In other words, Viaud was now sufficiently confident of what he had done on A by himself not to want to abandon it, but not sufficiently invested in the project, or sure of himself as a writer, to undertake the fusion of the two revisions himself. Jousselin tried – this meant undoing parts of his revisions to B – but when the navy told him to prepare for a new assignment, he turned over both A and B not to Viaud but to Émile Aucante at Calmann-Lévy, asking him to pull everything together. Viaud, who had been willing to let Jousselin consolidate A and B, was not happy with this arrangement. On 24 February he wrote to Aucante asking him to disregard B altogether and use A as the copy text. 'I don't want anything [in A] to be changed by anyone other than me, – not even by my friend M. Jousselin,' he added, dismissing B as 'the bad *Béhidgé*'.[2]

In a little less than a year, Viaud had gone from being happy to write a novel 'together with' Polignac to wanting full control of his creation. He would continue to ask Jousselin for help with future manuscripts, but Viaud had now assumed the role of confident verbal artist. In the end, the published novel, *Aziyadé*, would retain aspects of both manuscripts.[3]

Meanwhile, on 8 March Viaud wrote to Hakidjé and yet another friend and fellow officer, Pogarritz, who was stationed in Constantinople, pleading with the latter to help the former escape from her harem and come to France. He closed his letter to Pogarritz with the no doubt unintentionally ironic remark: 'Don't be afraid that you're getting involved in an adventure from some novel; this isn't one' (*Journal I*, 459). By this point in his complex life the difference between novel and reality had become tenuous. After having written those letters, Viaud spent the night with Pierre Le Cor, a handsome, muscular sailor who had become his latest Joseph Bernard/Daniel 'brother'. Le Cor would be the model for the central figure in Viaud's novel *My Brother Yves*. But while Viaud could pursue all these lives simultaneously, it is better if we hold off on his relationship with Le Cor until later in this chapter.

The attempt to get Hakidjé out of her harem and into Viaud's arms failed. Twenty-some years later, when a similar project did succeed, the author would discover just how much trouble it caused him in France.

While he relived his Eastern loves through text revisions and letters to Hakidjé, Viaud developed a sentimental life in France as well. As he wrote to one unhappy object of his only-momentary affections at the end of the summer: 'I have had ravishing mistresses in the past; I have some now and will have some in the future. That is perhaps easier for me than for other men, because I'm not like everyone else' (*Journal I*, 522).

Still, even Viaud had limits. Early in October, while he was correcting the proofs for *Aziyadé* and seeing some of his ravishing mistresses and thinking about Hakidjé and Joseph Bernard and Pierre Le Cor, he took time out and spent several days in a Trappist monastery in Normandy. In the diary entry describing this stay he recalled King Solomon's line 'Vanity of vanities, all is vanity' from Ecclesiastes, one of the books attributed to that king with seven hundred wives, many foreign, and three hundred concubines (*Journal I*, 526). Did Viaud feel a sense of kinship?

The last major publishing issue that had to be settled was *Aziyadé*'s author's name. Because he was an officer in the navy, Viaud would have needed written permission from his commanding officer to publish a book with his name on it, unlike the drawings that had appeared in magazines over the previous several years. For reasons we do not know, he decided against this at the last moment and opted for anonymous publication. Did he fear that he had said too much about himself? Did he have second thoughts, too late, about having kept passages that Jousselin had removed from manuscript B on moral grounds? A week before the appearance of the novel, Viaud wrote to Jousselin: 'all my plans for the future are summed up in two concentrated cyanide capsules that I'm going to buy with great difficulty' (*Journal II*, 35). Jousselin took this seriously and told him that 'there is always a remedy for everything.' Others might accuse Viaud of overdramatizing. On 21 January 1879, Calmann-Lévy, one of the leading publishing houses of what was then the artistic capital of the world, brought out the first edition of a novel by a new but unknown author: *Aziyadé*. No one committed suicide.

In fact, not much of anything happened. Few critics bothered to review it. One who did, Maxime Gaucher in the *Revue politique et littéraire* of 22 February, declared that the main character was 'a lieutenant in the English Navy who probably never existed, any more than his tender friend Aziyadé' (*Journal II*, 43). In light of the fact that the novel would subsequently be read as little short of pure autobiography, as for example by Lesley Blanch, this is amusing.

After Viaud made a name for himself – or at least for Pierre Loti – *Aziyadé* became one of his bestsellers. By the end of his life in 1923, it had gone through 201 regular editions with Calmann-Lévy, plus several beautifully illustrated ones.[4] The novel gained new notoriety in 1971 with Roland Barthes' preface for an Italian translation, an essay subsequently published in French and later English in Barthes' *Nouveaux essais critiques* (New Critical Essays).[5] The French literary theorist proclaimed that *Aziyadé* was a modern text because it went against the tradition of nineteenth-century French novels in several respects. It dealt with homosexuality without moral censure. It incorporated modernist techniques that exploded the traditional unifying narrative voice – not surprising, since one of the precursors of literary modernism, Gustave Flaubert, was Viaud's favourite novelist. In this last respect *Aziyadé* was, Barthes declared, much like the *nouveaux romans* (experimental new novels) then coming out of France for which Barthes had provided a theoretical foundation.[6]

One could object that Barthes saw in Viaud's first novel some of his own preoccupations more than what was actually there. As we will see when we get to *Iceland Fisherman* and *The Story of a Child* in the next two chapters, however, that sort of self-discovery was what Viaud was crafting his own art to facilitate.

In 1978 Edward W. Said, a professor of English literature at Columbia University, provided a new direction for Anglo-American academic literary criticism with his *Orientalism*, an encyclopedic study of how the West has misrepresented the East.[7] It gave rise to dissertations pointing out the Orientalist, and then Africanist, Japonist and so on, misrepresentations of other cultures in nineteenth- and twentieth-century Western literature, literature created at a time when few Westerners had the objectivity to see the cultural biases that informed their views of these cultures. (Said's own first scholarly work was on Loti-admirer Joseph Conrad, one of the most Orientalist of major Western novelists.) Because these dissertations are often the work of scholars-in-training – rather than specialists who have spent years becoming familiar with the corpus of the authors with whose colonialist works they deal – they sometimes exaggerate the elements on which they focus and do not deal with other, less biased aspects, much less the authors' other works. Particularly unfortunately in the case of Viaud, the books that have grown out of some of these dissertations have positioned him as a colonialist writer, when, as we shall see, almost all of his major works, those upon which his reputation is based in France, are set in France itself.[8]

Though Said mentions Viaud only twice and never *Aziyadé* by name, the novel, when dealt with since by some of these academics, has been swept up in this tide of scholarly denunciations. It is true that the novel has Orientalist features. A careful reading, however, shows that it was remarkable for its time in presenting Constantinople's (male) Turkish inhabitants as possessing a tolerance for difference that fundamentally changed, for the better, its Western protagonist in ways that his closed-minded European homeland had failed to achieve. (Barthes had already remarked in 1971 that the novel is as much a condemnation of Western moralizing as a hymn to Oriental freedom.)

A more justified criticism of the novel could be made by feminists. Harry Grant does not mistreat Aziyadé, but neither does he or Viaud accord her much opportunity to speak with her own voice. There is no attempt to see the story through her mind. We are told that she adores Grant, just as he adores her, and that pretty much defines her character. Viaud would improve on that, and radically so, when he wrote his other novel about women in a Turkish harem, *Les Désenchantées* (The Disenchanted),[9] almost twenty years later, but in the interim he would produce several popular novels in which the female object of desire is little more than that.[10] Despite this, his work had a particular success with women, including some very intelligent and independent ones. As Michael G. Lerner observed, Viaud 'captured the hearts of an audience that was largely feminine'.[11]

Though initial sales of *Aziyadé* were not impressive, Calmann-Lévy gave Viaud a contract for another novel. The author returned to the Normandy Trappist monastery for 'a few days of peace and contemplation' (*Journal ii*, 38–9). Perhaps inspired by his conversations with a group of men who had accepted celibacy as a way of life, Viaud decided to derive his second novel from his diary entries on Tahiti, which since French explorer Louis-Antoine de Bougainville published his account of the island in 1771 has been known in the West as the New Cythera – a land of beautiful and constantly available young women where you do not have to work to eat or make love.

Viaud had to work at this project, however, in a way that *Aziyadé* had not required. Whereas he had had 140 pages of diary entries to call upon for his story of Salonica and Constantinople, his few short weeks in Tahiti had left him with less than a third of that. Furthermore, whereas there had been a real, extended love story in the East with Hakidjé, Viaud, though he had spent time with young *vahines* while in Tahiti, had not had any great romance with one of them. He would have to invent one, and invent Harry Grant's Polynesian ardour for her.

The result, Rarahu, a beautiful fifteen-year-old from Bora Bora, bore a variation on the name of his brother Gustave's Tahitian 'wife', Tarahu. Amateur Freudians have been quick to jump on that, and probably not without reason. The fact that Viaud referred to his successive male love interests (however he understood and acted upon that love) as 'brothers' suggests that he had some sort of complicated fixation on the man whom he had viewed as the major male figure in his childhood home. Loving an imaginary woman who was a variant on Gustave's Tahitian wife may have been another way of loving Gustave.

'These are not memoirs like *Aziyadé*,' he wrote to Jousselin from Cherbourg a few weeks after having left the monastery, by which time he seems to have composed most of a manuscript. As he explained to his friend:

> Truth is respected only in the details [of the setting?]. The basis
> of the story is not true. I combined several real individuals
> to make one: *Rarahu*, who seems to me to be a fairly faithful
> study of young Maori women . . . The work you undertake will
> make something presentable out of this book, which would
> have remained incomplete as regards its form, like everything
> I do, if you hadn't put your hand to it. (*Journal II*, 44–5)

Despite his unhappiness just a year before with the way Jousselin
had radically redone *Béhidgé* without consulting him, Viaud once
again turned to his friend for help.

Jousselin made a lot of corrections, this time mostly stylistic.
According to Raymonde Lefèvre, who had access to the manuscript
and provides Jousselin's comments on the first 36 pages, Viaud
accepted most of his suggestions.[12] There were no arguments this
time about who could alter what. Viaud wrote the novel as sole
author. Jousselin limited his role to correction and did not try
to create or significantly censure. By 19 March Viaud reported to
his friend that Calmann-Lévy already had the manuscript with
Jousselin's emendations inserted and that he expected to hear
their decision the next day.

The result, Viaud realized, was not a tightly plotted traditional
novel in the style of Balzac, Flaubert or his contemporary Zola, but
the Impressionist in him did not mind that. As he wrote to one of his
new admirers, the wife of playwright Jules Sandeau, 'I only knew how
to jot down the deep impressions that I felt, reproduce the paintings
that nature put in front of my eyes – I don't have the talent of a writer'
(*Journal II*, 199). The talent of a painter to capture nature and the
feelings it awakened inside him, yes, that Viaud was convinced that he
possessed. It was, after all, what his sister Marie had counselled him
to attempt when he first started writing, as we saw in Chapter One.

It was also what Monet was doing. Having departed on a
painting excursion to Étretat on the Normandy coast, the artist told

his friend and colleague Frédéric Bazille that 'what I will do here
. . . will be simply the expression of what I personally have felt . . .
The older I get, the more I realize that no one ever dares express
honestly what he feels.'[13]

When the success of his second novel validated Viaud's
Impressionist approach to narrative, he decided to continue in
that vein. He informed another of his new admirers, the then very
esteemed and popular novelist Alphonse Daudet, that in the future
he hoped to 'bring together in one loosely knit volume a mass
of impressions experienced in the past in all the countries of the
world' (*Journal II*, 168).[14]

Intent on not having his second novel disappear like the first,
Viaud undertook what we would today call savvy marketing. He
had met Sarah Bernhardt while he was in the Paris area in 1875
to build his body. He now gave her a copy of *Rarahu* while it was
under consideration by Calmann-Lévy. The day after he signed the
contract, he reported in his diary that she complimented him on it
at her weekly salon, informing him that she had passed it around
among her friends.

Bernhardt was not the only woman who undertook to promote
the novel. Since the establishment of the initially shaky Third
Republic at the beginning of the decade, Juliette Adam had been
hosting a republican salon whose regulars included leading writers
(Hugo, Flaubert, Daudet) and political figures. Earlier in 1879 she
had founded a review, *La Nouvelle Revue*, that featured essays on
politics and the arts plus new literary works. Her goal, and no
doubt that of her politician husband, was to create a left-of-centre
republican outlet that could give prominent voice to ideas not
acceptable to the established and more conservative *Revue des deux
mondes* (Two Worlds Review).[15]

Like other salon leaders, she wanted to present herself as the
sponsor and mentor of new artistic talent, so she was particularly
intent on publishing works by as yet unknown but promising

authors. When she asked Calmann-Lévy if he had anything she might use, he showed her *Rarahu*. She was enchanted and convinced the publisher to delay the novel's appearance in book form so that she could debut it in instalments in her *Nouvelle Revue*. In the process she also convinced the publisher and Viaud to change the title to *The Marriage of Loti*, which it has borne ever since. Adam published the novel anonymously as 'by the author of *Aziyadé*', which, given Viaud's first book's lack of success, was not a strong selling point.

But sell it did. On 15 March, when it appeared in bookshop windows, *The Marriage of Loti* proved to be an instant, astounding success, both with the critics and the public.[16] Viaud admitted to his diary that he had not expected such a triumph, and was pleasantly surprised by the extra advance against future royalties that he received only four days later. He was particularly pleased that Alphonse Daudet wanted to make his acquaintance. When they met, Viaud reported that Daudet told him he had not seen anything in French literature in the last fifteen years that was the equal of *The Marriage of Loti*. That was hyperbole, of course, and Viaud would have realized it. Those fifteen years had seen the first publication of masterpieces such as Flaubert's *L'Éducation sentimentale* (A Sentimental Education), the first part of Zola's *Rougon-Macquart* series, including *L'Assommoir* (The Drunkard), and several of Daudet's own best works.

Still, the 29-year-old who three months before had been an obscure naval officer had every reason to feel on cloud nine. Soon there would be *Loti* candy and *Rarahu* ribbons. Juliette Adam would inform him that 'many people now write only in a Tahitian style, ending their letters with "I have finished my little speech, I send you greetings"' – a reference to Rarahu's letters to Loti in the novel.[17] *The Marriage of Loti* was presented at the French Academy in 1880, evidently for some sort of prize. Paul Gauguin, who was hunting for an exotic place that would help him distinguish his work from the Impressionists, read it on the recommendation of his friend Van Gogh and ended up spending the rest of his life in French Polynesia.[18]

Though a great success in its day, the novel is likely to strike modern readers as less interesting than *Aziyadé*. It comes closer to the exoticist cliché of the Western man who has a fling with a 'native' girl in some exotic setting but then leaves her forever when the fleet sails – though Harry Grant does feel guilty about having left her: he has nightmares about Rarahu's ghost laughing at him accusingly. Like Aziyadé she dies because he leaves her, though in a less romantic way: once he departs, she goes from sailor to sailor, contracting a venereal disease and dying of that rather than a broken heart as Aziyadé had done. Like her predecessor in the first novel, she is perhaps the work's least interesting and developed character. There are wild tribal dances around nocturnal fires, superstitious fears of sacred places and much of the rest of the exoticist clap-trap that Hollywood would still be recycling even after the Second World War.

On the other hand, Queen Pomare IV appears every bit as intelligent and astute as any European diplomat. The novel also bears witness to, and bemoans, the fact that the indigenous Maori culture was dying, being replaced by aspects of European civilization imposed in particular by the missionaries, foreshadowing James A. Michener's *Hawaii* eighty years later. Though Viaud does not go into that extensively, it was a major problem from whose nefarious effects today's Tahitians are still trying to recover.

The novel does introduce a new theme, seldom reprised by those who recycled Viaud's colonialist formulas, that will play an important part in some of the author's best work and that should redeem this one somewhat in feminists' eyes. Unlike Aziyadé, who does not have much of a voice in the first novel, Viaud presents Rarahu as a very accomplished singer and song composer who knows how to give expression to the nature around her in admirably complex musical creations. This artistry is not depicted as just a simple natural gift for which she deserves no individual credit, like a songbird. Rather, the narrator repeatedly presents her songs as artfully composed – even today, Tahitian polyphony is remarkably complex. Rarahu is inspired by nature, certainly, but she is an accomplished artist in her own right who works at conveying that inspiration in a crafted work of art. This, too, was very much how Monet understood art and his creation of it.[19]

On 3 April the new darling of the Paris literary world, whose real name was still unknown to most of his now numerous admirers, set sail on the *Friedland* for his first voyage outside France since he returned from Constantinople. With him he took a contract from Calmann-Lévy for the next six years – and a sense that he could, in fact, become the successful artist that had long been his goal, even if it was to be with words and not oils.

Once again Viaud decided to mine his diary for material, specifically his Senegal sojourn. There was somewhat more content regarding that than there had been for Tahiti, since he had lived in Africa longer. Again, however, there was not the making of a book-length romance, at least an exotic one with a 'native' girl, since Viaud's romantic preoccupations in Senegal had been with the European woman and Joseph Bernard. Still, he had already fabricated one such romance from very little with great success, so he had no reason to doubt his ability to pull another rabbit out of that same hat. The first ports of call for the *Friedland* were on the Algerian coast, moreover, so that gave him a chance to relive some of the African atmosphere he wanted to put in his third work. In particular he wanted to capture the light, as Monet did there and virtually everywhere he painted.[20] He wrote to Daudet that 'this manuscript will bring you a little bit of sunlight' (*Journal II*, 157).

The Marriage of Loti – and now *Aziyadé*, which had started to sell because of it – were doing so well for Viaud that by 13 May he was able to celebrate having paid off the debt on the house in Rochefort. He had Jousselin remind him every hour 'with the regularity of a cuckoo in a clock': 'You don't have any more debts!' (*Journal II*, 186).[21]

When he returned to 'terrible heat' in Toulon in September, finishing *The Story of a Spahi* on the 9th, he noted in his diary that the book was 'almost entirely written' in his apartment there (*Journal II*, 238–9). That may explain why the novel speaks constantly about the sun and the heat. It also suggests, as we will see, that Viaud was coming to require appropriately evocative surroundings for his narrative creations.

While the manuscript was being considered by Calmann-Lévy, Viaud continued on the *Friedland* for its autumn campaign in the Adriatic. When not occupied with his duties onboard, he had romantic interludes with young women at various ports of call. He also continued to submit illustrations of places encountered during the voyage to *Le Monde illustré*, but started to change the name with which he signed them. A depiction of the fleet in Ragusa's harbour that appeared in the 25 September 1880 issue was signed 'Monsieur Z., our special correspondent', rather than J. Viaud or Julien Viaud as in the past. The 2 October issue explained that the text that had described that depiction had been omitted from the previous issue for lack of space and that it was by 'Monsieur Loti'. But that same issue also offered a Viaud drawing of the fortress at Dulcigno that was again attributed to 'Monsieur Z . . ., our special correspondent' (*Journal II*, 780–81). The text was the first prose Viaud published under the name Loti, which suggests that he was considering coming part-way out of anonymity as a prose writer. The rest of the illustrations that appeared that autumn in *Le Monde illustré* were all signed Loti.

This new signature implied several things. First and most obviously, Loti – which in *Aziyadé* and *The Marriage of Loti* was a nickname for the Englishman Harry Grant and did not have the first name Pierre preceding it – did not die in the Battle of Kars in 1877, as reported at the end of the first novel. He was still alive in 1880, drawing and writing and evidently still in the navy, but the French one. Second, he wrote in French and so was, perhaps, the author of the diary entries attributed to Harry Grant in the first two novels. That would mean that, third, and *pace* that reviewer of *Aziyadé*, there was probably at least some truth to Loti's amorous adventures in Constantinople and Tahiti. Fourth, the fact that he wrote in French also meant that Loti was most likely French and not English, which suggested that, fifth, not everything in the first two novels about the Englishman Harry Grant was true. Loti had gone from an apparently fictional character to a living man of considerable mystery and some artistic talent in both words and drawing.

By 27 December 1880, Viaud was back in Toulon, working on the 'last corrections' for his African novel, *The Story of a Spahi*, with Jousselin, whom he had once again asked for help (*Journal II*, 297). After the work appeared serialized in *La Nouvelle Revue* during the first half of 1881, Viaud asked Juliette Adam to send the jointly corrected manuscript back to him 'because of my friend Plumkett's [Jousselin's] annotations' (*Journal II*, 335).[22] Viaud still wanted to be able to keep track of who had contributed what to his prose work.

On 24 February 1881, Viaud was finally promoted to lieutenant, the rank his protagonist Harry Grant holds in *Aziyadé*. This put him in a largely administrative position for the next few years, so he was able to spend his time in France, often with his ageing family in Rochefort. When he arrived there on 6 March, he recorded in his diary: 'They are so happy, the two poor old ladies [his mother and aunt], to think that they will keep me with them a long time, like a bird in a cage' (*Journal II*, 330). This meant a return to restrictive middle-class provincial France for the now world-travelled and morally liberated Viaud, who had derided those Western restrictions in *Aziyadé*. It therefore also meant it was time to play another role, that of the dutiful, moral Protestant son, 'this character that I play for [my mother], named Monsieur Viaud, officer in the navy, a well-behaved and fairly proper young man' (*Journal II*, 341).

There was an escape hatch on that cage now, though, one purchased with the success of his novels. Starting in 1877, even before he had paid off the debts incurred by his purchase of the family home, Viaud had begun, to the extent that his finances allowed, to transform his deceased great-aunt Berthe's bedroom into a 'Turkish room'. Though he would continue to develop it in years to come, by 1881, thanks to the royalties from *The Marriage of Loti*, Viaud had made a lot of progress. As he recorded in his diary on 1 June 1881:

> When I am all closed up in my Turkish room, when the scented harem pellets are burning, when the old weapons shine against the dark background of the old hanging rugs, – my thoughts depart for the East . . .
>
> My orderly Clarac resembles my poor little Mehmet. I have him dress as a Turk in an outfit that Mehmet wore. And when he is on the floor in front of me, lighting the water pipe, I dream about my house in Eyoub [where he had lived with Daniel and Hakidjé in Constantinople], and my heart tightens strangely . . . (*Journal II*, 338)[23]

He even had a professional photographer take a picture of him in Turkish attire in that room, which he sent to friends.

If this room allowed him to imagine himself far from Rochefort when he was there, he also took a certain amount of pleasure in considering how the townsfolk, who had known him and his family through their worst economic times, now had to eat their once hurtful words. In the same entry that spoke of his séances in the Turkish room, he rejoiced: 'I have money, and I will always have it . . . I've become a personage, at least to an extent, even for the closed-minded bourgeois of my birthplace – Who would have said that, a few years ago?'

Loti, in Turkish attire, in his Turkish room.

In March, April and May *The Story of a Spahi* appeared in *La Nouvelle Revue*, again as an anonymous text, this time 'by the author of *The Marriage of Loti*', which was a selling point. On 13 September the novel was published by Calmann-Lévy. Once again it was a great success, both critically and financially. On the cover appeared an author's name: Pierre Loti. It was not much of a disguise. Later that month *Le Figaro* published an article revealing the identity of this new literary sensation.

By Viaud's death in 1923, *The Story of a Spahi* had gone through 101 editions. Today, however, it is perhaps the most difficult of his works to read. The Senegalese men are often portrayed as handsome and noble, but the women, who again have no real voice of their own, come off too often as savages, with no exceptions like Queen Pomaré IV. Jean Peyral's affair with one of them, Fatou-Gaye, is presented as degrading, very much unlike Loti's marriage with Rarahu or affair with Aziyadé. There are some beautiful descriptions of the desert and an honest consideration of the effects of heat and isolation on European men not used to them. Viaud told Juliette Adam – when he was asking her to serialize it in the *Nouvelle Revue* – that 'I will probably never write a more powerful book than this one' (*Adam*, 10). Still, if there is any one Viaud text I would be happy not to read again, it is *The Story of a Spahi*.

It is easy to understand why it would have sold in its day, though. Like the other major sea-going powers of the era, France had developed an overseas empire in the seventeenth century. By the early nineteenth century, however, because of military defeat or financial exigency, it had lost almost all of it. When Napoleon III proclaimed the Second Empire in 1852, he decided that France needed something more than northern Algeria and a few scattered remnants of its old colonies to justify that new claim to world prominence. The liberal Second Republic had put an end to slavery in the French colonies in 1848, and so eliminated the purpose of the French slave trade outposts along the West African coast. In

1854, however, Napoleon III appointed Louis Faidherbe to expand what had been one such post, and by 1865 Faidherbe had extended French control to most of the western bulge of the continent. (Viaud was involved in the 'pacification' of internal tribes during his assignment there in 1873–4.) At the same time France began taking control of Indochina, a topic to which we will return in the next chapter. Because French incursions into western Africa were still in the news in the early 1880s, including articles in the big illustrated periodicals, *The Story of a Spahi* had an already existing market of French readers curious about what these new colonies might be like.

With his three tales of love in exotic lands, Viaud created a niche for himself in literature. Indeed, those three novels created a perception of his work that survives well over a hundred years later, though it does not take into account most of his subsequent, better work and now operates largely to his detriment.

He still had years to run on his six-year contract with Calmann-Lévy, so his only problem was deciding what to write next. Once again he turned to his diary, but with very different results. To understand them, we need to back up to Viaud's return from Constantinople in 1877 and examine the biographical thread that we could not cover then.

At the end of 1877, by which time he had left Toulon for the naval base in Brest, Viaud wrote to Jousselin, who was then suppressing 'immoral' passages in *Béhidgé*, that he had re-established contact with a Breton quartermaster his age, Pierre Le Cor, whom he claimed to have known for some time.[24] 'It's fun to have a comrade who accepts all your ideas with admiration and takes you for a man of genius,' he informed his friend. Viaud theorized more abstractly about this later when he told fellow author Émile Pouvillon: 'complicated natures like ours relax when in contact with simple natures' (*Journal II*, 336).

Le Cor's alleged simplicity or naïveté was not the only thing that made him appealing to Viaud. As he detailed in a diary entry

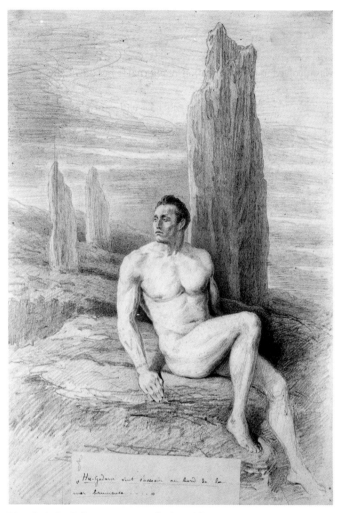

Pierre Loti, *Hu-Gadarn Came to Sit on the Shore of the Foggy Sea, January 1878* – a drawing of a nude Pierre Le Cor as a Celt.

Hôtel Continental, Paimpol.

devoted to the Breton sailor, the young man had 'the arms of a Hercules, muscles of iron . . . When Pierre takes off his clothes, you would say he's a Greek statue [with] the powerful lines of an antique athlete' (*Journal I*, 415–16). Viaud had used some of this language before to describe his objects of desire, but the fascination with muscles was new.

He incorporated it and Le Cor into his and his nation's already existing mythology about the Bretons. Viaud convinced this descendant of the Celts – who, as we saw in Chapter Four, were being glorified in art at that time as France's best, most powerful and noble ancestors – to pose for him naked as a Druid leaning against a menhir (a megalith).[25] The legend on the drawing reads: 'Hu-Gadarn sits along the shore of the misty sea'.[26] Viaud's time knew of this supposedly gigantic Celtic bard through a literary forgery, Iolo Morganwg's *Third Triads*, which were a Welsh equivalent and contemporary of James Macpherson's equally forged ballads of the non-existent ancient Scottish bard Ossian. Le Cor was not, therefore, simply another in the line of handsome 'brothers' that began with Joseph Bernard, though he was that as well. He was, or at least could be presented in art as, a contemporary embodiment of the ideal Frenchman, a modern descendant of the Celts who exemplified at least the physical traits that late nineteenth-century France was attributing to his ancestors and trying to foster in his male contemporaries in preparation for the next, inevitable war with Germany.[27] Pierre de Coubertin, the Frenchman who founded the modern Olympics in 1896, was a product of this same mentality.

In February 1878 Le Cor decides to take the train to Paimpol to visit his mother, who had moved back to Kergrist, a village to the west of that town, after the death of her husband in Saint-Pol-de-Léon. Viaud tags along. When they reach Paimpol they take a room at the Hôtel Continental, where Viaud had stayed when he landed there with Joseph Bernard ten years before. It is raining, and Viaud prays in his diary: 'May the rain continue until tomorrow; in that case Pierre won't leave until tomorrow morning and will sleep tonight in Paimpol with me' (*Journal I*, 424). The weather does not cooperate, however. 'Unfortunately it's no longer raining,' he reported later. 'Pierre will leave' to see his mother.

Viaud tries to hold on to him. He arranges for a late supper so that, at its conclusion, it will be too late for Pierre to set off for Kergrist. And the only available room in the hotel has just one bed! Viaud undresses and climbs in first. 'Pierre gets undressed slowly and without conviction.' What does that mean? 'I see that he is still hesitating,' Viaud wrote in the present tense, since the scene was evidently still present to him when he recorded it. '"Stay here, brother," I say. "I'm chilled to the bone . . ." "No," he says, "no. You see: I need to go and see my elderly mother . . ." And he quickly put his coat back on' and left, walking the several miles to Kergrist that night (*Journal I*, 426).

That this diary entry survived the censure of Viaud in late life, as well as of his son and moralistic daughter-in-law, is amazing. That

Viaud included it in his fourth novel, *My Brother Yves*, even toned down, is well past amazing (*Yves*, Ch. 15). That *My Brother Yves*, in which Pierre's feelings for Yves Kermadec (Pierre Le Cor) constitute the only real love story, turned out to be one of Viaud's bestselling novels – going through 207 editions by the author's death, more than any of his three preceding narratives – is flabbergasting. The only thing yet more remarkable is that there have been biographers like Lesley Blanch who read the diary and still adamantly maintained that Viaud was heterosexual.[28]

Le Cor developed 'conviction'. By the autumn of 1879, Viaud recorded in his diary that he and Pierre had spent the last year 'in a fraternal intimacy every moment, living together day and night', though not without 'storms between the two of us' (*Journal II*, 107–8). As with Joseph Bernard and Daniel before, this relationship, whatever else it may have been, involved deep affection. Viaud confided to his diary that 'our affection has grown a great deal in the last year . . . the thought of leaving each other for the unknown is very cruel for both of us' (*Journal II*, 108). Viaud did not hesitate to interpret Le Cor's feelings for him, as he had done for Aziaydé and Rarahu and Joseph and Daniel in the past. This fear of being separated from regular contact with Le Cor recurs regularly in the diary after that. By the end of 1880 they are sleeping together in the same bed when stationed in Toulon.

As with Joseph Bernard in Tahiti and Senegal, this deep affection also inspired in Viaud feelings of domesticity. As often in the past, he preferred to take an apartment on shore when he was in port for some time. He did so while he was stationed in Brest and invited Le Cor to share it with him. By April 1878, he reported that the officers on board the *Tonnerre* who had been with him in Constantinople already 'say on board that I've found the Eyoub of Brest!', the part of Constantinople where he had lived with Daniel and Hakidjé (*Journal I*, 463). Like the ones who encouraged him to publish his diary account of his adventures in

Constantinople, these officers do not seem to have been bothered by Viaud's non-standard living arrangements, nor he by their apparently moderate kidding. He did not feel a need to argue that he and Le Cor were 'just friends', much less to hide that they were living together, this time without a Hakidjé. By mid-May Le Cor and Viaud are addressed as *Monsieur* and *Madame* at a small-town hotel where they stop to dine regularly, and even this does not appear to bother Viaud (*Journal II*, 64, 443). When they are together on the *Friedland* in 1881, he writes of Le Cor spending all his evenings with him in his 'boudoir with a distinguished and mysterious luxury' (*Journal II*, 321). In French, *boudoir* is specifically a woman's bedroom.

This relationship, whatever its exact nature, was not free of discord, just as those with Joseph Bernard and Daniel had not been. The diary contains repeated mentions of arguments, some very serious, some that made Viaud fear everything was over. Things always got patched up, however.

This relationship continued for the four years covered by this chapter and *My Brother Yves*. In July 1880, Viaud accompanied Le Cor to St Pol de Léon in northwest Brittany when Le Cor wanted to recapture memories of his childhood. The episode, including three church steeples seen from a moving carriage, would figure not only in the Viaud novel but, like other elements in that work, in Loti-fan Marcel Proust's *In Search of Lost Time*, also devoted, as its title suggests, to recapturing the past.[29] Viaud also subsequently helped Le Cor buy a house in what is now central Rosporden, a house in which, Le Cor promised, one bedroom would always be reserved for Viaud – just as Viaud had reserved a room in his Constantinople house for Daniel.

Since she had not understood her younger brother's attachment to Joseph Bernard, it is not surprising that Marie Bon was troubled by Julien's affection for the socially inferior Le Cor. 'I don't detest him,' she assured her brother in a November 1881 letter; 'perhaps

I would appreciate him better if you told me what he has done to you [*ce qu'il t'a fait*] that you love him so much.[30] This time Viaud did not write back to deny that he was in love.

Viaud reproduced almost all of this – the happy moments, the arguments, and even some of the declarations of love – in the manuscript he set about extracting from his diary for Calmann-Lévy. A few of the most clearly homoerotic moments, such as the hotel bedroom scene in Paimpol, he toned down but usually did not omit. The biggest changes are not what Jousselin would have termed moral, but rather artistic. The author, who was by then taking himself seriously as a literary artist, moved a lot of the passages around to create a narrative arc which his relationship with Le Cor did not have. Pierre was already married to Marie Anne Le Dauff when Viaud met him in 1877, for example. His namesake in the novel, Yves Kermadec, does not announce his upcoming nuptials to Pierre, the narrator and Viaud stand-in, until a third of the way through the narrative. That creates trauma for the Viaud character that could not have happened, at least as such, in Viaud's real life. Other events are moved around or distanced from each other in a similar fashion so that the story stretches from 1874 to 1883, whereas the real events had occurred in half that time.[31] Viaud had already done something similar in *The Marriage of Loti*, as we saw.

If this affective thread was enough to fill a novel, it was not enough to keep Julien Viaud fully occupied. In October 1881, he went to Lille for his first meeting with Joseph Bernard since the latter left Senegal in 1874. If Viaud's short diary entry is to be trusted, they got along well and went back to addressing each other as 'brother'.[32] Perhaps because Senegal was on his mind, perhaps for other reasons, Viaud that month also went to see his son from that era, the child of the woman who had gone to Geneva, and found him to be a good-looking and hearty boy. Viaud makes no mention in his diary of the mother, who evidently no longer interested him. On Christmas Day 1881, Viaud received a letter from Constantinople informing him that Mehmet was dead but saying nothing about Hakidjé. He dreamed of returning to find out, as Harry Grant does at the end of *The Marriage of Loti*.

Also that October Viaud took his mother and Marie's daughter Ninette to Paris for several weeks of theatre-going. While there he wrote in his diary:

> It's an all-consuming life for me to arrange time to take them around and lead my own life, the life of Pierre Loti, and, when I get home at night, to finish the series of instalments I'm writing for *Le Temps*. (*Journal II*, 350)

He does not specify what leading the 'life of Pierre Loti' entailed at that moment, but it is almost certain to have involved some strand or strands of romance. This had become the life of Pierre Loti (as distinct from Julien Viaud, 'a well-behaved and fairly proper young man'): a seemingly endless series of romantic adventures at least a few of which were carried on simultaneously. Pierre Loti experienced no shame when some of these adventures were not of a traditional middle-class nature, or even necessarily heterosexual. He was someone interested in having sons, yes, but not really interested in having a permanent wife. Above all, Pierre Loti was a man freed of virtually all western European culture's moral restrictions, like his alter-ego Harry Grant in *Aziyadé*. From now until the end of Viaud's own life, this was to be the life of Pierre Loti.

Viaud could not always live that life himself, at least when he was required to be Julien Viaud in France. (If that reminds you of Jack's explanation to Algernon that 'my name is Ernest in town and Jack in the country', from Wilde's *The Importance of Being Ernest*, I'm happy.) He could, however, live it through the alter-ego he had now christened, and would spend the rest of his life developing. Viaud would nevertheless sometimes acknowledge to himself and close friends that, as fascinating as he might be, Pierre Loti was, in the end, a fiction. He concluded a letter to Jousselin with the assurance that 'there is nothing fake [*factice*] in this letter, nothing of Loti' (*Journal II*, 376). Whether Viaud always made that distinction no one can tell.

6

The Writer Becomes a Self-conscious Artist (1882–6)

Viaud even came to wonder if he could play all his roles without their collapsing on top of him. To Mme Blanche Lee Childe, one of several female intellectuals who became a fan of his first books and then a trusted correspondent, he wrote about

> this scaffolding of faults and lies that will fall on top of me one day . . . Where am I going, my God, carrying on three or four personalities at the same time under different names, tricking, being tricked? How will I finish up? (*Journal II*, 549)

Sometimes the structure did collapse, at least in part.

On 11 April 1882, for example, he writes in his diary of 'the terrible threat that is hanging over my head from the direction of Geneva . . . My life, my honour, everything is in question – It seems that I've reached the final hour for earthly punishments, that I have no future' (*Journal II*, 392). A week later that danger seems to have been put to rest, but again there are no specifics. He writes of 'that terror that was coming from Geneva . . . I am saved, but I no longer have a son. I seem to have committed some new infamy there by abandoning him so that they will leave me in peace' (*Journal II*, 394). There are seldom specifics in the diary, but such entries make it clear that their author spent a lot of time worrying that one of his personalities' actions were going to come to light and get Julien Viaud into trouble.

Kreizker bell tower, Saint-Pol-de-Léon.

Not everything was sombre for him, however. Royalties from his first three novels continued to pour in. In January 1882, Viaud entered into discussion with Jousselin about writing a sort of philosophic dialogue together, which became *Fleurs d'ennui* (Blossoms of Boredom). It contains the first appearance in Viaud's published writing of Pierre Le Cor. The character Loti opens the work by recounting to Plumkett (Jousselin) a recent dream. He and

Yves (Pierre Le Cor) had climbed the Kreizker chapel bell tower in Saint-Pol-de-Léon when, suddenly, the tower collapsed. Loti then saw Yves, bigger than ever, 'clothed like a Celt, with wolf pelts thrown over his shoulders'.[1] In 1882 Viaud still saw Le Cor and the Bretons whom he had met through him as modern incarnations of the original and best French, the Celts.

This understanding shaped his next novel, *My Brother Yves*, which he mentions to Adam in July 1882 as 'this Breton novel' (*Journal II*, 416). He tells her that 'I lack courage to write it,' no doubt because he had decided to tell the story of his love for another man as directly as he dared in late nineteenth-century France. By January 1883, at which point he is well into writing it, he informs Blanche Childe that it is a book 'in which I have put and am putting a great deal of my life' (*Journal II*, 453). To his friend Émile Pouvillon he expressed fear that it was too close to autobiography, 'maybe too faithful to be turned over to the public, because [the tableaux I present in it] represent the person whom I love the most in this world'.[2] At other times that self-revelation seemed to entice him. In the letter to Juliette Adam quoted previously he asserted that 'I only know how to unveil [*dévoiler*] my intimate nature and my feelings about life' (*Journal II*, 416). For someone who had written a novel about women living behind veils, *Aziyadé*, someone who was still telling his diary at the end of 1882 that he and Le Cor got a kick out of being called 'monsieur and madame', the use of the verb 'unveil' does not seem to be abstract or random (*Journal II*, 443). One can almost imagine Viaud seeing himself as some sort of very complex Salomé; it is almost as if there were a feminine element in him that wanted to perform that dance, and a conservative element that hesitated. After Viaud's death, his legitimate son Samuel and a family friend wrote that 'Loti . . . wanted to be made out [*deviné*] under his mask and got irritated that he was not. Timidity? Shame? The need to be *deviné* tormented Loti his whole life.'[3] Viaud's – and certainly Loti's – life involved a series of masks or veils that he put on but then wanted to remove, and perhaps wanted others to watch him remove.

He took the writing of *My Brother Yves* very seriously. As Bruno Vercier explains in his critical edition of it, Viaud developed a detailed outline that was almost half as long as the novel itself.[4] He constructed the story as a series of tableaux, like a stroll through an art gallery, rather than as a continuous narrative. When he sent an early version to Pouvillon for comments, he called it 'a *pêle-mêle* of photographs'.[5] Several of the reviewers, all positive, spoke of the novel as a collection of paintings.[6]

If Viaud's view of inland Brittany was, in certain respects, frozen in a sort of mythological time, the other subject of *My Brother Yves*, his relationship with Pierre Le Cor, remained as unstable as ever. He had once told Pouvillon that 'the *me* that is deepest inside me, the real one, is a primitive man' so he was happy that the equally primitive Le Cor understood him. Now, however, he complained to Jousselin that, while Le Cor still held 'first place' in his heart, 'there is a whole part of me that he does not understand and that he disdains. He is the *simple me*'s brother' – but that was no longer enough (*Journal II*, 406).[7] Viaud wanted someone who could understand him in all his complexity as well. Still, when Le Cor talked about sailing with the navy to the colonial wars in Southeast Asia late in 1882, Viaud did not want him to leave. As he wrote in his diary: 'I was afraid that I loved him less, but I see that I love him with all my heart, and that he loves me as well' (*Journal II*, 443–4). Though he did not see it yet, part of the problem was that, as Viaud fell in love with new people, men as well as women, he did not fall out of love with previous beloveds. This, too, made his life very complicated.

My Brother Yves appeared in serialization in August and September 1883, and then in book form from Calmann-Lévy, another great and instant success. By Viaud's death it had gone through as many editions as his first three novels combined.

Most of what makes the novel of potential interest to readers today has been discussed in the previous pages. It is perhaps the first positive, centralized depiction in modern French literature of a man's love for another man. Balzac had presented Vautrin's love for several adolescents in an ambiguous fashion in *Le Père Goriot* (Old Man Goriot) and several other novels, but he never let us forget that Vautrin, a secondary character, was a criminal. Flaubert had toyed with the presentation of the giant Mâtho's relationship with his crafty servant Spendius in *Salammbô* – supposedly Viaud's favourite novel – but Mâtho was a barbarian during the Punic Wars and not a modern-day Frenchman.

Viaud dared to go much further. There is nothing 'wrong' with Pierre, who loves Yves, nor anything wrong with Yves except that he drinks too much. Unlike in *Aziyadé*, moreover, Pierre has no affairs with women, though Viaud had no shortage of heterosexual affairs during the period on which he could have drawn if he had wanted to make Pierre's interest in Yves more ambiguous. The idea of homosexuality, and therefore of sexualities – that every individual has an innate attraction to one sex or the other and that that attraction is part of her or his central makeup – was just starting to take hold in the western European scientific community at this time.[8] How aware of that discussion Viaud may have been in the early 1880s it is impossible to say. It is not impossible to say, however, that with Pierre in *My Brother Yves* Viaud created one of modern Western literature's first gay central characters.[9] What makes this all the more interesting is that Pierre is not, in this respect, a carbon copy of his creator, though they are close enough in other respects to have left many readers wondering. Parts of the French press were soon using the phrase 'brother Yves' to refer to a gay man's lover. Marcel Proust, who had admired Viaud's work since his adolescence, used parts of *My Brother Yves* in constructing the first section of his own autobiographically based narrative about an ambiguously gay man, *In Search of Lost Time*.[10]

Paul Iribe, cartoon in *L'Assiette au beurre*, 25 April 1903.

The other interesting aspect of *My Brother Yves* is that Viaud made Yves Kermadec's drinking another of the central issues of the novel. There are also scenes of drunken urban dwellers around the harbour in Brest that focus on how alcohol has reduced them to the dregs. It is therefore not surprising that one of the novel's early reviewers, Firmin Boissin, described the work as 'the *Assommoir* of seamen', a reference to Émile Zola's 1877 novel about the effects of alcohol on the poor in contemporary Paris.[11] Viaud does at times give the impression in *My Brother Yves* that he is a naturalist studying the wretched lives of the poor, especially the urban poor, in the style of his contemporary Zola. There is definitely a distance between the narrator, Pierre, who comes from a middle-class background, and most of the Bretons he meets. Pierre is never dismissive or disdainful, as the narrator sometimes is in *Germinal*, for example, Zola's masterpiece about the miserable life of contemporary French coal miners. Neither does Pierre see himself as one of these Bretons, however, even when he puts on a Breton costume to participate in their festivities or learns some of their language. He is too busy observing them and their customs to see them as his equals. That will change, and drastically, in Viaud's next, also Breton, novel, *Iceland Fisherman*.

Viaud was on his way to Indochina by the time he completed the last section of *My Brother Yves* in May 1883. During the voyage he made friends with another Breton sailor, Pierre Scoarnec, who was 'taller and had broader shoulders than my cabin door; terrifying arms, as hard as mine, but much larger' and yet displayed 'the manners, vocal inflections and candour of a little child' (*Journal II*, 489). Scoarnec would become the model for young Sylvestre Moan in *Iceland Fisherman*. Viaud became very attached to him, comparing him to Le Cor.

As part of his quest to establish an empire of world significance, Napoleon III, shortly after sending Faidherbe to West Africa, made use of an attack on Jesuit missionaries in Indochina to conquer territory there. In the decades that followed there were sporadic rebellions, however, and French repression of them. When Viaud arrived in early August 1883, he heard about a massacre of civilians by French soldiers that had taken place just before his arrival as part of the capture of the forts at Thuan An outside Hué, then the capital. He wrote a long article about it and sent it to the Parisian daily *Le Figaro*. That widely circulated paper printed the first three installments on the front page in late September and October, the first two anonymously, the third with the name Pierre Loti. The anti-colonialist Parisian press, led by Georges Clemenceau, lauded Viaud for his courage and called for a reconsideration of the government's colonial policies. The English, German and even American press decried the barbarity of the French military. Despite the law of 29 July 1881, which had guaranteed the French press its first real freedom, the government censured the article. The continuation announced at the end of the third instalment never appeared. On 2 December 1883, Viaud learned that he had been called back to France and was at risk of court martial.

Since by now he saw himself as a career naval officer and prized that, he was terrified. He wrote to Juliette Adam, asking her to intercede for him with her friends in high places and assuring her that his article had been misinterpreted. This was disingenuous. To his friend Oirda he had written earlier how senseless he found the government's colonial policies. Near the end of his life, in *First Youth*, after he had retired from the navy for the last time and was free to speak as a civilian, he condemned the French role in Indochina, decrying the war as an 'absurd and mad expedition' launched by 'one of the most nefarious of our governments' (*Youth*, Ch. 12). The article in *Le Figaro* paints an unambiguously gruesome picture of Frenchmen gone 'mad'.

On 6 February 1884, by then back in Paris, he was pardoned by the navy so that he could continue his career as an officer.[12] Madame Adam had pulled powerful strings, but it was also hard to cashier so well known a public figure. Viaud's fame would provide him with a protective shield for the rest of his career in the navy, much to the aggravation of some of the top brass.

In an article he had written for *Le Figaro* while still in Indochina that was never published, Viaud had concluded with the vow that, if he had to choose between being a writer or a naval officer, 'Pierre Loti will cease writing and existing, that's all there is to it' (*Journal II*, 503). It was a very dramatic stand, perhaps written with the hope of getting his large public to put pressure on the government or at least make the government fear that pressure. In fact, it toppled in April 1885, and with it its colonial policy in Indochina.

The end of his already-quoted letter to Juliette Adam from 9 December suggests that Viaud's mind was not quite so resolute about abandoning his career as a writer – but then she was his publisher, so he would not have told her anything that might upset her in a letter in which he was asking her to intervene to save his other career. The still unanswered questions are why he allowed *Le Figaro* to put his name on the third of the three instalments, if in fact that was his doing, and whether he really imagined the trouble this article would cause him when his identity was ferreted out. His adult life is the story of a man who often failed to look before he leapt.

Viaud was given an administrative appointment in France to keep him out of further trouble. This allowed him to spend the rest of 1884 and the first part of 1885 in Rochefort, installing the six hundred kilograms of baggage he had brought back with him from the East in some of the rooms he was transforming into time-travel machines linked to his voyages. By June 1884, he was able to hold a reception in one of them. Some of his female guests were dressed in Oriental style. He wore one of the costumes from his Constantinople days and had his orderly wait on them in similar attire.[13]

He also travelled around France during this period. Sometimes it was to visit Le Cor in Rosporden or an unnamed fisherman's daughter north of Paimpol with whom he had fallen in love during his trips there to visit Guillaume Floury – another large, handsome, muscular sailor in whom he had taken an interest. More often, it was to Paris, to which his ever increasing celebrity called him

Alice Heine, formerly Princess Alice of Monaco, Duchess of Richelieu, with Loti in the garden of his home in Rochefort *c.* 1910.

more and more often. On 12 May 1884, during one of these Paris sojourns, he was introduced to yet another female admirer, the Duchess of Richelieu. Born Alice Heine in New Orleans in 1858 to French parents involved in European banking, she was raised in France. There she married the Duke of Richelieu, as whose wife she held a salon famous for the writers and painters who attended. (Proust took her as the model for the Princesse de Luxembourg in *In Search of Lost Time*.) After the duke's death she married Prince Albert I of Monaco. (Their great-grandson, Prince Rainier III, would marry another American, film star Grace Kelly.) As Princess Alice of Monaco she played a great role in fostering the arts in the principality, in particular the Monte Carlo Opera, which in her time became one of the most important companies in Europe. She was also a sophisticated art connoisseur.

Through Daudet, Viaud also met Edmond de Goncourt, to whose work the novelist had previously introduced him. Invited to Goncourt's apartment one day with Daudet, Viaud was impressed with his collection of Japanese *objets d'art*. Goncourt was, in fact, one of the experts on Japanese art in the Paris of his time and would eventually publish important studies of Kitagawa Utamaro (1891) and Katsushika Hokusai (1896), perhaps the two Japanese artists who most influenced Monet.[14] When Viaud found himself in Japan a year later, he would start by viewing the island through the Japanese art he had seen in Goncourt's home.

On 14 February 1885, Daudet invited Viaud to dinner at his home with Goncourt and one other friend, the by then famous – and infamous – naturalist novelist Émile Zola. In his diary Viaud noted that 'they talked until two in the morning' (*Journal II*, 578). It had been a very full artistic and intellectual day for Viaud, since he had divided the daylight hours between Sarah Bernhardt and the Duchess of Richelieu, so it is understandable that he did not stay up still later to record what the four novelists talked about into the small hours of the morning. A certain amount of speculation is both permitted and required here, however, because this dinner and others that followed seem to have played a major role in shaping *Iceland Fisherman*, on which Viaud had been working for almost a year at that point and which he would subsequently rework entirely.

Though Viaud did not record the content of that long discussion, his admirer Henry James did write about his attendance at similar dinners in that same company a decade before. Because James at that point was in somewhat the same position as Viaud in 1885, a commercially successful author who wanted to become a great writer as well, it is worth considering what James got out of those conversations, to which Peter Brooks devoted several chapters in his *Henry James Goes to Paris*.

When James attended these literary soirées in 1875, they were still dominated by the novelist both he and Viaud admired the most: Gustave Flaubert. Flaubert died in 1880 just as Viaud started to make a name for himself. James called the group a 'council of Gods' whose intelligent and fascinating discussion of literary art made James feel as if he were on top of Olympus.

> there is nothing more interesting to me now than the effort and experiment of this little group, with its truly infernal intelligence of art, form, manner – its intense artistic life. They do the only kind of work, today, that I respect.[15]

For Viaud, who had already been working on issues of form with Jousselin as early as *The Marriage of Loti*, dining with this group must also have seemed like a trip to Olympus. He had already experimented in *My Brother Yves* with some of the modernist techniques developed by Flaubert and Goncourt – and then James – like free indirect discourse and, with it, sudden shifts in perspective. Raymonde Lefèvre has shown that in his remarks on the *My Brother Yves* manuscript Jousselin made comments that gave rise to extensive discussions of style and form with Viaud.[16] Viaud would pursue these issues and techniques more extensively in *Iceland Fisherman*, which, not surprisingly, James hailed as 'to my sense perfect'.[17]

One thing that evidently did not come out of these *dîners à quatre* was an increased inclination towards naturalism. *My Brother Yves* had shown much influence by Zola and his largely negative view of the poor. *Iceland Fisherman* repeats none of that, and in fact is constructed in part as a refutation of *Germinal*'s largely derogatory depiction of the working class.[18] By 1891, when Viaud was chosen over Zola to join the French Academy, he used his acceptance speech in part to criticize the naturalists for their exaggeration and negativity in depicting the nation's poor. We will examine that speech in Chapter Eight.

On 26 January 1885, a few weeks before this first *dîner à quatre*, Viaud had informed his diary that he was hastening to finish the 'last dark chapters' of *Au large*, the provisional title he had given his second Breton novel (*Journal II*, 577). He had evidently been working on it since at least 23 April of the previous year, at which point he had announced that 'I count on this new book more than on all the others' and asked Juliette Adam for her opinion on it, which would suggest that even then it was already substantially under way (*Adam*, 35). By 12 February 1885, two days before the *dîner à quatre*, he had evidently finished it, because in his diary he mentions reading it with Adam after having dinner with her. Since Viaud had not had to serve on any naval expeditions since his return from Indochina in January 1884, he had had a full year of largely uninterrupted time to work on it, more than he had devoted to any of his previous works.

And yet, he would not turn over the last, completed part of the manuscript to Adam for more than another year. Why? Why did he suddenly no longer see it as ready for publication? The next time he mentions it in his diary, on 3 March 1885, he sounds as if he is starting over almost from scratch: 'I'm working on constructing *Au large*, which is giving me a lot of difficulty . . . In the past I wrote my books as the wind blew [*au hasard*], pushed by I don't know what need to write down my impressions' – the last few words being a phrase he had used in years past when talking about his previous work (*Journal II*, 582). 'The opinion of the public was secondary for me.' Now, evidently, the opinion of the public, some public, did matter to him, and he was willing to work to earn it. Which public? His sales had been better with each of his preceding novels, the reviews favourable as well. That public liked what he had been doing already. To what extent was the public whose opinion he now coveted those three men with their 'truly infernal intelligence of art, form, manner – its intense artistic life', the ones who were doing 'the only kind of work, today', that Henry James, but perhaps also Viaud, 'respected'?

One aspect of Zola's approach to literature that had not particularly interested Viaud previously now became important to him. Just as Zola had spent several days around Anzin in northeast France so that he could give a very detailed, documented depiction of the coal miners' daily lives in *Germinal*, suddenly Viaud, in March 1885, having been working on *Au large* for a year, informed Juliette Adam that he was trying to get assigned to an expedition to Iceland so that he could produce 'a more beautiful book' (*Adam*, 52–3). Still the painter at heart, Viaud was striving for beauty like Monet and did not mention truth, which was Zola's watchword and indeed the concept over which he and Monet fell out around this time.

Viaud was sent not to Iceland but back to Indochina, where the French were still carrying on their 'absurd and mad' war. In his next letter to Adam he assured her that 'I hope to have a considerable success without [the trip to Iceland]. I'll leave Iceland as a strange, distant vision and concentrate on the sea and Brittany,' suggesting that he intended to rework the novel considerably (*Adam*, 54–5). He also told her that he intended to show what he had already written to Daudet, a member of the 'public' that now mattered to him. To put himself in the mood to work, he informed Adam, he focused his thoughts on the fisherman's daughter from Ploubazlanec, whom he still loved and whom he had given the name Gaud (Marguerite, in Breton) in his text. At this point Viaud was evidently still thinking of writing about the love of some man, perhaps Pierre Loti, for a poor, uneducated fisherman's daughter, rather in the style of *Aziyadé* or particularly *The Marriage of Loti*. That is not what he ended up publishing, however.

While in Indochina he re-established contact with Pierre Scoarnec, who was the primary model for Sylvestre Moan in *Iceland Fisherman*, and Pierre Le Cor, with whom he resumed an emotional relationship. In *Iceland Fisherman*, though Sylvestre resembles Scoarnec physically and, to the extent that we know, emotionally, Viaud gave him Le Cor's matriculation number, 2091, so for the author there was something of both men in the young sailor. Like Proust's *In Search of Lost Time* a generation later, *Iceland Fisherman* is populated by characters whom Viaud created by fusing elements of different acquaintances, and aspects of himself.

The war against China did not go as quickly as the one against the Annamites two years before, so the French gave their ships and crews periodic breaks for rest and relaxation. In July they sent the *Triomphante*, on which Viaud and Le Cor were serving, to Nagasaki for what turned out to be four months. Imagining a life for himself there à la Pierre Loti, Viaud confided to his diary that

I will rent a little house made of paper, in a suburb, amidst gardens. I will be surrounded by flowers. Then, I'll take a little (female) friend with a cute doll's face, with beautiful black hair combed in a funny style. In the evening, Pierre [Le Cor] will come to our house and keep us in line. (*Journal II*, 605–6)

It was exotic romance as Viaud understood Pierre Loti, with Le Cor a welcome third. It was also, at least at first, Japan as he had imagined it through the *japoneries* he was accustomed to seeing at Goncourt's Paris apartment. When he first arrives in the archipelago, he views everything in terms of the Japanese engravings he had known back there, even though many of them presented a distorted or at least exaggerated view of the land. This is not as odd as it may seem. As Jan Walsh Hokenson has shown, some nineteenth-century French were so convinced that the Japanese drew what they saw without modifying it to suit artistic convention that they believed Japan actually looked as it appeared in that art.[19]

The Japanese sojourn turned out to be a loveless send-up of a Pierre Loti adventure. Viaud 'hired' a wife, Okané-san – 'out of boredom and loneliness', he told his niece – and set up a household with her in the hills overlooking Nagasaki (*Inédite*, 195). If this sounds familiar, it is because the novel that Viaud developed from it two years later, *Madame Chrysanthemum*, would become one of the three sources for Puccini's opera *Madama Butterfly*.[20] Even the novel was not so romantic, or so tragic, however. In neither does Loti make any pretence of loving the young woman, nor does he imagine that she loves him. The only suggestion of love occurs when Le Cor starts living and, eventually, sleeping with them, at which point Loti becomes jealous. In this sense, the novel turned out to be a send-up of Viaud's first two Loti-falls-in-love-in-an-exotic-setting romances, filtered through the Pierre–Yves relationship in *My Brother Yves* with its episodes of jealousy when Yves marries Marie.

If Japan was the site of Viaud's loveless 'marriage' to Okané-san, it was also the cherry-blossom-strewn decor for a sort of second honeymoon with Le Cor. While they were together there Viaud wrote: 'We understand each other better, more deeply. I think we love each other even more than before, in a more confident, more serene, more rational way' (*Journal II*, 655). The only cloud on this horizon was that Viaud was suspicious about Le Cor's feelings for – and activity with – his Japanese bride.

During this sojourn Viaud developed an appreciation for Japanese art. His diary starts to speak of it as 'the height of elegance made with nothing, refined simplicity', and he takes trips around the islands to study particular examples of it (*Journal II*, 627). When he first arrived in Nagasaki he had informed Juliette Adam that 'I will never have the courage to write a Japanese study; that would bore me too much,' thinking, perhaps, of Goncourt's current project (*Adam*, 70). In the end, however, he wrote a novel set in Japan whose principal interest, at least for those likely to read it today, is not its sham marriage but rather its commentary on Japanese art and Viaud's use of that commentary to speak about Monet-style Impressionism, which was greatly indebted to it.

This appreciation for Japanese art and Impressionism had more immediate results as well. It shaped *Iceland Fisherman*, the text on which Viaud worked during his time in Japan. From Yokohama on 15 October 1885, after two months on the islands, he informed Juliette Adam that

> my novel . . . is giving me a lot of difficulty. I would like it to be so simple, so simple, so different from the insipid school and the gibberish that is invading us. [Notice the fascination with the simplicity he had found in Japanese art, and perhaps a reference to the naturalist school, with Zola's fondness for technical dictionaries and vocabularies such as one finds in *Germinal*, of which, as already noted, Viaud constructed *Iceland Fisherman* as a critique.] I would like to achieve extreme poetry in extreme, uncultivated simplicity. I hope to send you the first part [of *Iceland Fisherman*] at the end of the month; you will receive it in mid-December. (*Adam*, 74–5)

Viaud had gone back to the beginning of the novel and was rewriting it again, this time with a focus on artistic simplicity. A week later he told Adam that he was still working on Part One, but added: 'The novel is completely constructed, completely written. It just remains for me to arrange the descriptions, to finish them up, and then to recopy everything' (*Adam*, 75). 'Completely written' here did not mean complete. Viaud still had months of work ahead of him. But it was 'completely written' to his mind because the canvas had been laid out, the background of a sort, the form. He still needed to work on all the details, which are what would turn that background into a real work of art, but for him that was now secondary to the general form and structure, the things that so preoccupied Daudet's 'little group'.

This is also how Monet worked by then. He built up his paintings from quickly made initial colourings, often in a fashion that disguised the work involved to retain an air of spontaneity. He told the American painter Lilla Cabot Perry that

> the first painting should cover as much of the canvas as possible, no matter how roughly, so as to determine at the outset the tonality [colour scheme] of the whole . . . The one golden rule from which Claude Monet never departs, is to work on the whole picture together, to work all over or not at all. Neglect of this leads to loss of all harmony.[21]

Viaud, like Monet, would continue to follow this practice for the rest of his life.

Some of the rewriting of the early parts of the novel must have introduced the radical change in the Gaud Mével character, from the simple daughter of a poor fisherman, evidently loved as Rarahu had been loved before, to the Paris-educated, fashion-conscious daughter of a rich shipbuilder whose love for Yann Goas, far more than his feelings for her, occupies the central place in the novel as we have it. In fact, this time it is the man who seldom expresses his thoughts. Rather, he becomes an enigma, the object of Gaud's desire, which is presented as the almost always frustrated pursuit of an ever-changing and fleeting nature. In this respect, the romantic couple of *Iceland Fisherman* is an inversion of those on which Viaud had built his initial fame. They are more than just a romantic couple, though: they, and in particular Gaud, provide Viaud – yes, the names are almost identical, and not by chance – with an opportunity to discuss the goals and frustrations of the modern artist pursuing what was coming to be known as modernism. Like Flaubert and some of his 'little group', Viaud with *Iceland Fisherman* would, among other things, write a novel about art, and modernist, Impressionist art in particular.[22]

In this respect not only *Madame Chrysanthemum* but also *Iceland Fisherman* benefited from Viaud's stay in Japan and his reconsideration of Monet-style Impression in conjunction with Japanese art. He facilitated this by bringing back with him from Japan what he described in his diary as a 'terrifying load of baggage!' To display it all he transformed one of the rooms in the Rochefort house into a Japanese pagoda (*Journal II*, 649).

All the way back from Southeast Asia Viaud worked on what Juliette Adam had now christened *Iceland Fisherman*. He kept working on it into March in Rochefort while he constructed the pagoda. He was still working on it, to Adam's dismay, as the deadline for the first instalment in *La Nouvelle Revue* loomed. This man who had once been happy to turn over revision of his work to friends was now asking his editor if he could make further revisions to what he had already sent her. Somehow the first instalment made it into the 1 April issue, and the others in bi-monthly succession after that. Still, even with the serialization under way Viaud informed Adam in May that 'unimaginable complications' had him continuing to rework the last part. Later that month, finally, he wrote to say that he was about to undertake 'the last *vernissage* of Yann and Gaud', using the art term to describe the final preparation of a painting before it is sent off to the gallery for exhibition (*Adam*, 86). It had taken him almost two years to complete *Iceland Fisherman*, far more than any of his previous works. It was very much, for him, not just a work of art but a painting or series of paintings, what he had dreamed of doing for a living since he was a boy.

He was not the only person who held it in such high esteem. While it was still appearing in *La Nouvelle Revue*, the French Academy awarded him the Prix Vitet, including five thousand francs, for the totality of his work, none of which before *Iceland Fisherman* could really be described as great art. The last instalment appeared in *La Nouvelle Revue* in June, as did the book form, published by Calmann-Lévy. The reviews were almost uniformly glowing. Sales were even better than that. By October Viaud was rejoicing that 'I now have glory; Calmann-Lévy is giving me fistfuls of money, a fortune' (*Journal II*, 735). *Iceland Fisherman* would quickly become not just Viaud's bestselling work but one of the great French publishing successes of the second half of the nineteenth century.

Iceland Fisherman is not simply a good read, though it is certainly that. It is a remarkably rich one. First and foremost, it shows Viaud developing a variety of techniques to paint with words as Monet was painting with oils at that time, perhaps the high point of French Impressionism.[23] (The last of what are today known as the eight Impressionist Exhibitions took place in 1886.) In addition, Viaud constructed his narrative in a manner that allowed him to present his ideas on such Impressionism and to provide an example of an Impressionist artist confronting the challenges of Monet's version of modernism.

Viaud also constructed *Iceland Fisherman* to critique and offer an alternative to the naturalist presentation of France's working poor, very specifically Zola's *Germinal*, which had been appearing in serialization when Viaud met Zola at Daudet's dinner in 1885.[24]

He also constructed it as a continuation of his critique of France's colonialist policies, at least in Indochina.[25]

On a more personal front, in *Iceland Fisherman* Viaud rewrote, in a sufficiently obvious way, the story of Pierre's love for Yves Kermadec in *My Brother Yves*, this time substituting for Pierre a woman, Gaud Mével, so that he could express even more directly his love for another man, Yann Gaos, another Breton giant who was a combination of Pierre Le Cor, Guillaume Floury and perhaps Joseph Bernard. In the process, he created his first strong, fully developed female character, a woman who defies the confining social mores of her provincial milieu to pursue the object of her love, like Viaud, but also to develop for herself an independence-giving profession, a point that Viaud stresses by contrasting her work in dress design with that of her elderly relative, Yvonne Moan, who washes others' clothes for a poor living. Marcel Proust, a great admirer of Viaud's work, would opt for an inversion of this inversion in *In Search of Lost Time* to express his love for Alfred Agostinelli, whom he transformed into the Albertine of several of his volumes. Yann Gaos also experiences a deep but never defined love for his fellow Iceland fisherman Sylvestre Floury, whom Viaud modelled on Pierre Scoarnec but also Pierre Le Cor. The novel therefore has no shortage of amorous and sometimes desiring gazes directed towards men.[26] This may explain why Michael Moon described *Iceland Fisherman* as 'perhaps the most pungently male homoerotic novel about a sailor before Jean Genet's *Querelle de Brest*'.[27] Still, *My Brother Yves* is both a more directly homoerotic work about sailors and the structural model for Genet's narrative.

Iceland Fisherman was also a major success with the general reading public, from the most discriminating on down. Ernest Renan, one of the great minds of the nineteenth century and a major proponent of Celtic culture, told Viaud, whom he would subsequently sponsor for the French Academy, that 'I have cousins and distant cousins who fish off the coast of Iceland like the men in your novel . . . You have painted them wonderfully.'[28] (Note, again, the comparison with painting.) At the other end of the educational spectrum, Viaud spent an evening in a Paimpol bar in September 1886, three months after the novel had started selling in bookshops. 'People surrounded me, bought me drinks: my book has been read and understood by all these fine men – who would have thought it? – and they love me for having written it,' the astounded Viaud recorded in his diary (*Journal II*, 734).

He was on the top of the world – at least for the moment.

7

Art, Memory and the Use of One to Highlight the Other (1886–90)

Since *Iceland Fisherman* provided Viaud with success both artistic and commercial, it is not surprising that he continued to work in the field of combined verbal and visual art.

To begin with, he continued dining with Alphonse Daudet and the latter's artistic brethren when he was in Paris. At least once a year for the next few years, his diary records a dinner with Daudet and often Edmond de Goncourt. It does not record the subjects of their colloquies, but again a certain amount of informed guessing is appropriate. Goncourt, whose Japanese *objets d'art* had caught Viaud's attention before he was stationed in that country in 1885, was still at work on what would eventually be published as a two-volume study of *Japanese Art in the Eighteenth Century*. He must have questioned Viaud about the country, which he never visited. Viaud may have wanted to talk about the art he had discovered there with a man who was one of the recognized French authorities.

Viaud makes no mention of seeing Zola at these dinners or elsewhere during the ensuing few years, but the naturalist was evidently not gone from his mind. He would use *Madame Chrysanthemum*, his novelization of his sojourn in Japan, to counter Zola's attack on Impressionism in his immediate post-*Germinal* narrative, *L'Oeuvre* (The Great Work of Art).[1] After its serialization in *Gil Blas* while Viaud was still in East Asia, that novel appeared in bookstores starting in March 1886, just after Viaud's return to Rochefort while he was finishing work on *Iceland Fisherman*.

Goncourt, who saw himself as the superior art expert, expressed in his diary real contempt for *The Great Work of Art* and Zola's presentation of artists in it. That may explain why Viaud appears no longer to have encountered Zola at the Daudet/Goncourt dinners.[2]

Viaud was working on his new, Japanese novel by 1 February 1887. From the start he envisioned an artistic presentation. There would be no initial serialization. To spite Calmann-Lévy, whom he accused of short-changing him on royalties, Viaud signed a contract on 5 March to bring out the work in the prestigious E. Guillaume et Cie. collection. This was a series of large-format, extensively illustrated, limited-edition tomes that included the latest work signed by Daudet, *Tartanin sur les Alpes* (Tartarin in the Alps), 1885. Viaud, who had once supplemented his officer's pay by illustrating his own and others' brief texts, allowed the Guillaume brothers to hire Joseph Rossi and Félicien Myrbach-Rheinfeld to do the 204 watercolours and drawings that adorn this edition, which was sold at three times the price of the standard editions of *Iceland Fisherman* and Viaud's previous novels. There was even a special one-thousand-copy numbered edition on fine paper with silk covers and a three-dimensional sculpture on the protective box by École des Beaux-Arts sculptor Alexandre Falguière. The sculptor had just recently completed a statue of the *Triumph of the Revolution* that still today crowns the Arc de Triomphe. That edition of *Madame Chrysanthemum* sold for fifteen times the price of the standard editions of Viaud's previous novels. In short, the Guillaume brothers pulled out all the stops to give Viaud's new work a very artistic presentation.[3]

Viaud at his end gave this work equally artistic attention. He composed it surrounded by the 'exquisite scents of spray after spray of roses and orange blossoms – sent continuously from southern France – magnificent big bouquets', trying to relive through his senses life in Nagasaki and make his readers experience that as well (*Journal III*, 50). (Had he read Joris-Karl

Alexandre Falguière, sculpture on the boxed edition of *Mme Chrysanthème* (1888).

Huysmans's *À rebours* [Against the Grain], the great Decadent novel, which had appeared in 1884 and included a chapter in which the protagonist, des Esseintes, has a 'perfume organ' created so that he can experience the effects of a wide range of delicate perfumes?) As he tells the art-loving Duchess of Richelieu in the dedication to *Madame Chrysanthemum*, 'it is quite certain that the three main characters are *Myself, Japan* and the *Effect* that the country had on me.' Though there is technically a male–female relationship in the narrative – a French naval officer whom we assume to be Pierre Loti but who is never named rents a wife, Mme Chrysanthemum, while stationed in Japan – there is no pretence of a love story, except to the extent that the officer-narrator becomes seemingly jealous when Yves appears to become involved with his wife. In his dedication Viaud asks the Duchess of Richelieu to accept the novel like any other strange work of art brought back from Japan.

There is no real plot, just a series of episodes involving the three main characters, rather like individual tableaux one encounters strolling through an art museum. Viaud had already experimented with this narrative technique in *My Brother Yves* and *Iceland Fisherman*, as we saw. He would have encountered it in some of the novels Goncourt had written with his late brother, like *Germinie Lacerteux*, two decades before. In *Madame Chrysanthemum* this impression was enhanced in the original editions with wide margins and extra white space between each episode, as if to suggest the white frames which several of the Impressionists were using at that time to set off their paintings.[4] Several of these episodes involve discussions of the Japanese art encountered by the narrator.

The real climax of the story has nothing to do with the title character, who is absent from the scene, but rather involves the efforts of the narrator to draw their house in such a way as to capture and convey not just the visual, but all the sounds and scents and feelings that he associates with it. (Remember Marie Viaud's and Monet's letters about making their viewers feel and taste what they had chosen to paint.) He finally realizes that he has to abandon a Western realist approach and adopt techniques found in Japanese art – and the sort of Impressionism Monet had developed in part from his extensive study of that art.[5]

How well did Viaud do? Vincent van Gogh, a great reader of contemporary French fiction, wrote to his brother Theo on 13 July 1888, a few months after the novel's publication:

> Have you read *Mme Chrysanthemum*? That description of the cloister or pagoda [in Chapter 40] where there was *nothing* (the drawings and curiosities all being hidden in the drawers) made me realize that the real Japanese have *nothing on*

their walls. Ah, that is how you must look at Japanese art, in a very bright room, quite bare, and open to the country.[6]

The novel is not perfect, certainly. The presentation of the Japanese, especially the women, is not generally flattering. (Viaud's highest praise is for his rickshaw driver, whose real-life name, Kikou-San, he gave to Chrysanthemum in the novel.) The book has therefore given rise to criticism from readers who found it racist.[7] But *Madame Chrysanthemum* is not about people, as Viaud explained in the dedication. To insist on reading it primarily for the romance is to impose a cultural bias of one's own, not to mention a disappointment. The work is primarily about art and one Westerner's discovery of Japanese art, almost but not entirely to the exclusion of the individuals and civilization that created it. That poses its own set of problems, of course, but the novel still merits an attentive reading not prejudiced by preconceptions, which is part of what it is about.

Despite the original, expensive formats – the novel was not issued in a standard, unillustrated Calmann-Lévy format until March 1893 – *Madame Chrysanthemum* proved to be another long-lasting success.[8] By 1923 it had gone through 221 regular Calmann-Lévy editions, more than any of Viaud's previous works other than *Iceland Fisherman*.

It is not surprising, therefore, that the next book-length project Viaud undertook was, once again, an art book. For this one, however, he did not rely on his diary; rather, he set off on an adventure that he could transform into a book and made sure he recorded it artistically in his diary. He took off to conquer not a woman, moreover, but a male artist. Not just any artist, furthermore, but the man who was coming to be regarded by Monet and some of the other Impressionists as the greatest painter of the first half of the nineteenth century. The painter who, among other things, has been forever since associated with republican France: Eugène Delacroix (1798–1863).

Though in his earliest work Delacroix had chosen subjects from history in accord with Academy teaching, he soon started to elaborate his version of Romanticism, moving away from Academic classicism in both style and subject-matter. In 1830 he produced his iconic *Liberty Leading the People*, a glorification of the 1830 revolution that overthrew the conservative Bourbon monarchy. It was bought by the state, only to be kept in storage until 1848 and the next, more republication revolution. Today its depiction of a bare-breasted woman carrying high the republican French flag while leading men of different backgrounds into battle is as well-known an image of liberty and equality as the (also French) Statue of Liberty.

In his *Essai sur l'inégalité des races humaines* (Essay on the Inequality of the Human Races, 1853–5), the anti-republican Arthur, comte de Gobineau had dismissed the Celts, the subject of two recent Viaud novels, as an inferior race. He proclaimed that the best Frenchmen were those descended from the Frankish nobles who invaded Gaul in the fifth century, conquering the Celts and driving some of them into remote regions like Brittany. By presenting the Bretons as the descendants and living manifestations of the 'first French', the Gauls, in *My Brother Yves* and especially *Iceland Fisherman*, which glorifies them, Viaud had asserted a republican stance on the nature of the French, in direct opposition to writers such as Gobineau.

After painting *Liberty Leads the People* and seeing it hidden by the new, still conservative French government of King Louis Philippe, Delacroix, disgusted,

traveled to Spain and North Africa, as part of a diplomatic mission to Morocco shortly after the French conquered Algeria [starting in 1830]. He went not primarily to study art, but to escape from the civilization of Paris, in hopes of seeing a more primitive culture [one of the reasons for Viaud's

Eugène Delacroix, *28 July. Liberty Leading the People,* 1830, oil on canvas.

fascination with Brittany]. He eventually produced over
100 paintings and drawings of scenes from or based on the
life of the people of North Africa, and added a new and personal chapter to the interest in Orientalism . . . He believed
that the North Africans, in their attire and their attitudes,
provided a visual equivalent to the people of Classical Rome
and Greece [as Viaud had found the Bretons of Rosporden
to be current manifestations of some prehistoric period].[9]

Delacroix believed that these North Africans could provide a
trip back in time far more interesting and useful to the artist than
just studying the art of antiquity and its imitators in museums,
as the Paris École des Beaux-Arts demanded that its students do.
There was everything here to appeal to Viaud: great art, travel
back in time, the social freedom of the Muslim world that he had
discovered in Constantinople.

Eugène Delacroix, *The Sultan of Morocco and His Entourage*, 1845, oil on canvas.

So, like Delacroix, he got permission to join a diplomatic mission to North Africa, in this case Jules Patenôtre des Noyers' 1889 excursion to further diplomatic relations with Morocco. (Had Viaud met Patenôtre in 1883 or 1885 when the diplomat was in Hué and Tonkin to negotiate the French protectorate of Annam?) The day after the birth of his first son, Samuel – we will come back to that later in this chapter – he set off across the Mediterranean to Algeria. There the scents reminded him of his previous North African sojourns, just as the roses and orange blossoms had put him in a Japanese frame of mind. Then on to the cities and towns of Morocco, not only those along the Atlantic coast like Tangiers that were more cosmopolitan, but inland to Fez and the 'real' Morocco.

Aimé Morot, illustration for Loti's *To Morocco* from *L'Illustration*, 21 September 1889.

The landscapes, to him, suggested what southern Gaul must have looked like 'in prehistoric times' (*Journal III*, 209). Everything he saw, smelled or heard as he crossed the desert or visited the cities he recorded in his diary, but far less the people, or at least individuals, than the desert landscapes and the urban markets.

He was setting up a competition with the best, with Delacroix himself. On more than one occasion in the travelogue he derived from his trip, Viaud chooses a scene depicted by his great predecessor and proceeds to describe it with a profusion of carefully nuanced and often vivid colours, rivalling Delacroix at his own game. Perhaps the best example is his description in Chapter Nineteen of the sultan's infantry lined up before the walls of Fez. It is hard when reading it not to think of Delacroix's *The Sultan of Morocco and His Entourage* (1845). It is equally hard not to think that Viaud wanted his readers to catch the reference and compare the two depictions, since someone chose this scene to be illustrated for that instalment of the travelogue when it was serialized in

L'Illustration. Aimé Morot's drawing makes very clear reference to Delacroix's masterpiece.[10]

Viaud not only rivalled Delacroix with words, he repainted the scene to make it more striking according to his own painterly aesthetic. While the robes of many of the men in the Delacroix canvas are of the same ochre colour as the city walls behind them, Viaud, like Monet at that time, focused on sharply contrasting colours that make each other that much more vivid against the neutral background of the surrounding crowds. There is no way of knowing what Viaud actually saw on 15 April 1889, how much he was reporting and how much he was inventing to compete with the Delacroix canvas. All he recorded in his diary for that event was one short sentence: 'Parade entrance into Fez' (*Journal III*, 222). Like the climactic drawing scene in *Madame Chrysanthemum* that he had developed from only the slightest record in his diary to present his Impressionist aesthetic, here Viaud seems to have created an elaborate descriptive scene so that he could compete with Delacroix. There is no winner; each artist was aiming at something different. Each produced a striking work of art in the process, however.

By May Viaud was back in Rochefort elaborating his diary pages into *Au Maroc* (To Morocco), his first travelogue. By August it began serialization in *L'Illustration*, where Viaud's relative Nelly Lieutier had arranged for the appearance of his first published artwork a quarter-century before. This time, however, the lavish illustrations were by Jean-Joseph Benjamin-Constant, who had himself travelled in North Africa and been influenced by Delacroix, and the lesser ones by Aimé Morot, a student of Cabanel at Paris's École de Beaux-Arts. After the conclusion of the serialization in October 1889, *L'Illustration* published the work in book form with the illustrations.[11] The next January Calmann-Lévy brought out a regular, unillustrated edition. It did not have the phenomenal success of Viaud's two previous art books, though it was on its 66th edition by 1923, which is still impressive for a travelogue. Viaud had more than once complained about not being good at coming up with a plot. Now he had proved that he could dispense with one altogether and still do what interested him most.

One new element in his life during this period was the increasing sudden eruption into his consciousness of memories from the past, in particular from his childhood. His diary makes more and more frequent mention of such eruptions through these years. He appears to have mentioned them to his friends as well.

One such friend from this period was Queen Elisabeth of Romania. Born Elisabeth of Wied to a minor German noble, she had attracted attention for her beauty – and her refusal to behave docilely – at the Prussian royal court. Queen Victoria considered her a good match for her eldest son, the future Edward VII, but 'Bertie' chose someone else and Elisabeth ended up in 1869 with Prince Karl of Hohenzollern-Sigmaringen, who three years before had been appointed the first Prince of Romania, a new principality in the already dying Ottoman Empire.[12] The Russo-Turkish War, during which 'Loti' had died in the last pages of *Aziyadé* fighting for the Turks, resulted in Romanian independence from those Turks. When Romania declared itself a kingdom in 1881, Elisabeth became its first queen.

Like the Duchess of Richelieu, she was no empty-headed socialite. Elisabeth had not simply an independent character, which led her to champion higher education for women in the kingdom, but also a love of the arts that focused on literature and led her to create both original works and translations into German of French texts. In 1887 she decided to do the first German translation of *Iceland Fisherman*, so she invited Viaud to the royal palace to talk about the project.[13] A few weeks after turning in the final revisions of *Madame Chrysanthemum*, Viaud caught the Orient Express and set off for Bucharest.

Because, with the opening of that part of the Orient Express just a few years before, Bucharest was close to Constantinople, once he

Elisabeth of Wied (1843–1916), Queen of Romania.

had finished with the Queen, Viaud caught the train there early on the morning of 5 October with the intent of learning, once and for all, the fates of Hakidjé and Mehmet. He stayed only three days, during which it was confirmed, first, that Mehmed had died – he kissed his grave – and then that Hakidjé was also deceased.

He discovered a great deal more than that, however. As he wonders around the city, astounded at how much of his life there over a decade ago comes back to him as he encounters familiar sights, Viaud, sounding very much like the Proust predecessor he was, marvels at how certain sensations, mostly visual but some auditory and olfactory, stimulate the unconscious part of the memory. He recalls episodes that he had left out of *Aziyadé* for artistic or compositional reasons and that had, as a result, vanished from his conscious memory. We do not just forget things, at least consciously, he comes to realize; our memories are also 'transformed' over time, in part by the very things, such as writing, that we undertake in an effort to preserve them. Art can stimulate memory, as Yann Gaos discovers in the central chapter of *Iceland Fisherman*, but the artist's efforts to transform his memories into a work of art, as Viaud had just finished doing with *Madame Chrysanthemum*, can transform them in our memory as well.

Viaud recorded all this very carefully, including many fine perceptions of the changing light over the Bosphorus, during his three days in Constantinople. Did he do so with the intent of turning it into another narrative that reflected on art and, this time, memory? He did not say, nor does he appear to have proposed the work to a publisher when he returned to France. Two years later, though, when Juliette Adam wanted a new work for *La Nouvelle Revue*, he mentioned the diary pages and she published his revision of them as *Fantôme d'Orient* (Phantom of the East), which Calmann-Lévy then brought out in book form in February 1892. It did not have the success of his novels: only 91 editions by 1923, though this was still very respectable. Still, it is fortunate that it was translated into English, because it is one of the most beautiful and thought-provoking of Viaud's works. It is often published, both in French and in English, in the same volume with *Aziyadé* as a sequel, which it is. Primarily, however, it is an extension of Viaud's reflections on the issues central to *Iceland Fisherman*, *Madame Chrysanthemum* and, to a lesser extent, *To Morocco*. It therefore reads more richly when contemplated after those. In his acceptance speech upon being elected to the French Academy Viaud would announce:

> It would, perhaps, be fortunate for a critic worthy of that
> name who needed to talk about a writer if he were to . . .
> read him . . . in the same order in which his books were
> written, and to follow in that way the development of his
> talent . . . and see take shape the sort of unity without which
> they can be neither great nor long-lasting. (*Speech*, 61)

That is true for the reader of Viaud's works as well.

The other result of his first meeting with Queen Elizabeth was his next novel of a sort, *The Story of a Child*. He had shared his flashbacks to childhood with her when he was in Romania, as their subsequent correspondence makes clear.[14] Thereafter she kept urging him to publish them. On 14 July 1889, he informed her that he had already written several pages of what he referred to as 'your book'.[15]

When he was elected to the French Academy a year after the publication of *The Story of a Child*, Viaud explained to those gathered in the Mazarin Palace to see him inducted that

> it doesn't matter to me if a book is called a novel or
> some other name – the only thing that I ask of it is to
> have life and charm. I disdain equally labels and rules,
> and I leave all disputes on the subject to hairsplitters
> who are themselves powerless to create. (*Speech*, 64)

This disregard for literary genre would have come as no surprise to anyone familiar with *Aziyadé, The Marriage of Loti, My Brother Yves, Madame Chrysanthemum* and *Phantom of the East*, all of which could be classified as novels, autobiographies or travelogues. As we saw, it was one of the things that made Roland Barthes acclaim *Aziyadé* as a forerunner of the New Novel. *The Story of a Child* is equally genre-defying, starting with its title. As we explained in Chapter One, '*roman*' in French means 'novel', the literary form. But it is also used when speaking of an event-filled life, especially a complicated one, which children do not normally have: *le roman de ma vie*, the story of my life.

The result is one of Viaud's most fascinating creations, whatever its genre. Sounding very much like Proust's nameless narrator a generation before the first volume of *In Search of Lost Time* appeared, the narrator of *The Story of a Child* explains that he does not intend to present an ordered, continuous narrative of his life, like a traditional biography or autobiography. Instead, he will only recount those events that struck him in a 'strange' way because they are connected to some sort of 'underside' in his mind (*Child*, Ch. 2). In doing so, he recalls episodes from his childhood which he crafts into reflections on the nature of Impressionist art and its role in activating the part of memory that Freud would soon be calling the subconscious. Impressionist art therefore serves a self-discovery function as well.[16]

Viaud had first presented these ideas in the central chapter of *Iceland Fisherman*, when Yann looks up into the North Atlantic sky and sees a vague form that, in his mind, takes the shape of his deceased friend Sylvestre, leading Yann to confront for the first time his feelings for the young man. In *The Story of a Child*, especially with the episode of the drawings of the Happy Duck and the Unhappy Duck in Chapter Nine, Viaud used what he presented as episodes from 'Pierre's' childhood to elaborate the full Impressionist aesthetic that lay behind his move to 'art books'. As with *My Brother Yves*, Proust made extensive use of this work in the first part of *In Search*

of Lost Time, another novel that seeks a different, more direct way
to recover memories of the past and, more importantly, the feelings
associated with them.

   The Story of a Child went through over one hundred editions by
1923. One of its first readers, Jeanne Proust, who followed it through
the pre-book serialization, had the advantage of commentary from
her eighteen-year-old son Marcel, who was reading it in those
initial instalments as well.[17] He would remember it very well some
twenty-odd years later when he set about transforming episodes
from his own childhood into the first part of what is probably the
greatest art novel in Western literature.

   Viaud tried to transform parts of his public life into works of
art as well, sometimes in startling ways. The first striking example
of this occurred at the lavish costume ball Juliette Adam gave in
February 1887. Precisely at midnight, once all the other guests had
arrived and impressed each other with their costumes, the Egyptian
god Osiris entered, attired in an astounding outfit that had taken
Viaud and his family a week to put together. He was so proud of
it that he subsequently went to a photographer's studio and had
formal pictures taken. The only problem was that Viaud was
upstaged in some of the women's eyes by the very handsome orderly
dressed in Turkish attire whom he brought with him. People
assumed he was Viaud's 'brother Yves'.

   If this was the first, it was not the last in a series of intentionally
outlandish public appearances that Viaud staged through most
of the rest of his life to create yet another public persona, another
aspect of Pierre Loti. He was someone who knew how to use the
new, large-circulation illustrated press through which he had first
appeared before the public to craft a persona – or personas – that
would, in their own way, be minor works of non-traditional, anti-
bourgeois art.

   Viaud proceeded to give equally lavish costume balls himself
when he inaugurated another fanciful room in his home in

Loti costumed as the Egyptian god Osiris, 1887, for Juliette Adam's masquerade ball in February of that year.

Rochefort. In October 1887, shortly after he returned from Constantinople, construction was finished on the Gothic Hall, a medieval dining room. (It replaced Marie's art studio.) On 12 April the next year he threw a lavish medieval costume ball with invitations in Old French and carefully researched food to match. The guests were requested to arrive in appropriate costumes and speak medieval French. Viaud assured wide coverage for the event: he invited a reporter and illustrator from *Le Monde illustré*, which had once published his drawings from exotic places around the globe, and had himself photographed in the costume he had created for it.[18]

Other costumed celebrations followed. On 8 November 1889, to inaugurate the new Turkish parlour and the serial publication of *To Morocco*, there was an Arabian festival. In March 1890 followed a production of Act IV of Ernest Reyer's new opera *Salammbô*, an adaptation of Viaud's favourite Flaubert novel, with Viaud evidently singing the part of Mâtho. Later that year Viaud staged a production of Act IV of Giacomo Meyerbeer's opera *Les Huguenots*, about the massacre of French Huguenots on St Bartholomew's Day 1572. (As mentioned in Chapter One, when Viaud thought about his Protestant ancestors, it was often in terms of the persecution they had suffered.) There was always a professional photographer present to capture the event for the public. Pierre Loti, his audience was learning, was a many-faceted individual.

If, unlike in preceding chapters, I have delayed Viaud's romantic entanglements to the end of this one, it is because, unlike in previous periods, those entanglements had little effect on his literary output. The least entangling of them was his marriage. On 13 June 1886, just as *Iceland Fisherman* was appearing in bookshops and stands, Viaud was introduced to Blanche Franc de Ferrière. He had asked his niece Ninette and her husband Gustave back on 14 February to find him a fiancée, posting his indifference to the subject by adding: 'I will allow myself to be led blindfolded' (*Inédite*, 221–2). Alain Quella-Villéger asserts that Nelly Lieutier

Medieval ball illustration, *Le Monde illustré*, 21 April 1888.

found this prospect, however.[19] On 20 October they were married. Viaud's comment in his diary that evening was: 'It seemed as if I were attending someone else's wedding' (*Journal II*, 739). The most famous comment on his marriage was written by playwright, actor and film director Sacha Guitry, who informed the world that 'The man was married, the sailor less so, Loti not at all.'[20]

Why did Viaud get married? He never explains it in his diary. It is unlikely to have been to quell rumours of his homosexuality; there were already enough more-or-less openly gay men in France who had wives for that not to have worked. His mother had been pestering him for years to do the conventional thing and get married; this would have put an end to that. Viaud also wanted healthy children, primarily boys, to carry on his line. Marriage was one, but as he discovered later not the only, way of obtaining those. As much as anything, I suspect, he wanted a full-time household manager now that his mother was getting elderly. The prosperous middle-aged writer needed someone to handle the day-to-day affairs of what was becoming a very considerable household. In November, back from their honeymoon in Spain, he confided to Marie that 'I hope I will find a little peace in my life, for lack of happiness, which is impossible' (*Inédite*, 221). Married life would not bring him peace, though, because he had no intention of giving up the life/lives of Pierre Loti.

While this marriage would be few modern Western women's ideal, it was not necessarily the worst of times in a nineteenth-century middle-class world where most women, in order to function in society, had to be married. Blanche came from a prosperous home; Viaud's ever-expanding income would guarantee that she could continue with such a lifestyle, one that included entertaining guests who would have been the envy of most Parisian hostesses, much less one who lived far from the capital. Viaud was absent from home often, as we have seen with his trips to Bucharest, Constantinople and Morocco, and did not object when Blanche chose to visit her family in Bordeaux or elsewhere. It was, in short, a marriage of convenience for both of them, something not uncommon in bourgeois France at that time. When she returns from a trip he bemoans his loss of freedom. On 5 December 1887, for example, he notes that 'poor little Blanche will be back in eight days, and I will take up my chain again, without end, without hope' (*Journal III*, 144). When he takes her to the train station so she can visit her family in Bordeaux, he walks back to the house slowly so that he can 'savour, deliciously, the three weeks of freedom and love that I have ahead of me' (*Journal III*, 156). She may have seen her absences in a somewhat similar light, if perhaps without the extra-marital infidelities.

Despite Viaud's fears after an early miscarriage that he would not be able to have children with Blanche, she gave birth to a son on 17 March 1889. The next day, as we saw, the author left for his trip to Morocco, according all of one sentence in the diary to his son's birth. Christened Samuel, the name of one of Viaud's persecuted Protestant ancestors – but also the first male love interest in *Aziyadé* – the boy was sickly as a child, which may explain why his father developed no attachment to him. By 14 June, when the boy was three months old,

Viaud admitted to his diary that his son 'still has not found any place in my life' (*Journal III*, 227). That did not change for years to come.

There were also the usual romantic adventures. On 9 February 1888, for example, Viaud waxes lyric about the 'sweet and cold marble' of the chest of one of these unnamed women on which he rested his head (*Journal III*, 155). Three months later, while riding through the woods near Rochefort, he has a 'sensual' encounter with a beautiful young gypsy. As Quella-Villéger and Vercier note, it is difficult not to suspect that these two real adventures had something to do with the unconvincing story of young J.'s sexual initiation with the statuesque gypsy in *First Youth* (*Journal III*, 168).

There were also romantic entanglements with men, some familiar names and some new. Viaud continued to see Pierre Le Cor on occasion, sometimes when he made his yearly trip to Rosporden to attend a *pardon* – a Breton religious festival – and visit his godchild, Julien Le Cor. Even in 1886 Viaud had told his diary that his affection for the Breton had been 'shaken up', but he did not abandon him, either emotionally or, when called upon, financially (*Journal II*, 727). He added Pierre Scoarnec, the handsome model for Sylvestre Moan, to his household staff.

The major new man in Viaud's life was the young sailor Léopold Thémèze, not a Breton but a Provençal. The author's relationship with him was different from those he had had with Joseph Bernard, Pierre Le Cor and other 'brothers'. Léo was both significantly younger than Viaud, by thirteen years, and described almost exclusively in terms of his 'godlike' physical beauty.[21] Bernard, Le Cor, Daniel in Constantinople and other 'brothers' had all been handsome, but Viaud had mentioned many other characteristics in his writings about them as well. They had existed for him as three-dimensional human beings. The first and often only thing Viaud remarks on when he refers to Thémèze is his evidently astounding physical beauty. Unlike with Bernard, Le Cor and Daniel, there are no records of arguments that lead to break-ups and then

Léo Thémèze.

reconciliations. At least in the diary, this appears to have been a much more peaceful relationship, perhaps because it was a more one-sided one. In November 1888, for example, Viaud describes Thémèze as 'this friend to whom I become more attached every day' (*Journal III*, 188). In the past, when speaking of Bernard, Daniel or Le Cor, Viaud had often written that they had loved *each other* more and more.

Thémèze is often in Rochefort and when there stays with Viaud, usually spending the night in the newly inaugurated Arab Parlour. When Blanche is gone, Viaud spends the night there too, with Léo on the floor beside him, just as Daniel had started out on the floor beside him in Salonica. After one of these nights in August 1887, Viaud tells his diary that when he can live with Thémèze like that 'I forget that I am married, I feel free and still young' (*Journal III*, 60). This was more the sort of relationship Oscar Wilde had with Lord Alfred Douglas than the stormy but relatively egalitarian ones Viaud had carried on with Bernard and Le Cor. Fortunately for Viaud, it never caused him the ruination that that relationship inflicted on the Irish poet.

8

Life at the Top (1891–1900)

The nature of Viaud's literary production changed significantly during the last decade of the nineteenth century. In the previous ten years, all the while serving as an officer in the French navy, he had established a reputation as an important fiction writer with six successful novels. In the century's final ten years Viaud published only two novels plus the short novel-autobiography-travel narrative *Phantom of the East*, which he had already drafted in his diary a few years before.

He also penned a three-volume travel narrative after a visit to the Holy Land and dozens of short pieces, most of them non-fiction, which he was able to sell to the nation's – and even England's – major newspapers, magazines and journals because of his ever-growing reputation as a popular but also serious author. A few are carefully crafted and some very moving. Most are just journalism. Their *raison d'être* seems to have been to help finance the purchase of houses adjacent to Viaud's in Rochefort so that he could continue to create elaborate time and space-travel rooms. The most notable of those during this decade was the mosque, the elements for which Viaud acquired in Damascus at the end of his travels though the Holy Land.[1]

What most enhanced his reputation as a serious author during this decade, especially in the eyes of those outside Paris's leading literary circles, was Viaud's election to the French Academy. Cardinal Richelieu, Louis XIII's chief minister, founded the

The mosque in Loti's house, Rochefort.

institution in 1635 to bring order and governmental control to the French language. Much of France has ignored its pronouncements ever since. Nonetheless, membership, which is for life, has usually been considered a distinction. The members are referred to as *les Quarante imortels* (The Forty Immortals); all forty chairs are seldom occupied at the same time, however, and many, if not most, of their occupants vanish into oblivion after their death. When one does shuffle off this mortal coil, the others elect a replacement.

In 1890, when Viaud decided to try to gain election, the major literary authors he knew personally, Daudet, Goncourt and Zola, were not members; the first two, in fact, were involved in founding an anti-French Academy that became the Académie Goncourt. Still, it is not surprising that Viaud decided to campaign for election (hopefuls had to campaign, making visits to the current members' homes and asking for their vote). He had started to take his writing seriously in the course of transforming his diary pages into *Aziyadé*. He had worked towards a more artistic, painterly style, particularly after meeting Daudet and his circle while he was creating *Iceland*

Fisherman. He had then continued in that direction with *Madame Chrysanthemum* and *To Morocco* and had employed *The Story of a Child* to theorize about his version of Impressionist art. As Joseph Bernard had predicted a decade before, Viaud was now 'paint[ing] for art and business', making a considerable success of it both artistically and financially. The French Academy had honoured him with its Prix Vitet in 1886. Why should he not have sought its greatest imprimatur, lifetime membership? He had, in fact, started to campaign for it at the end of 1889 at the suggestion of Daudet and Goncourt, but withdrew that application when a major politician, Charles de Freycinet, announced his candidacy.[2]

In 1890 his fellow candidates included four now-forgotten individuals and Zola, whose recent novel, *La Terre* (The Earth), of 1887, a fairly graphic description of farmers wallowing in physical and sexual depravity, had scandalized the more conservative French cultural scene. As a result, Viaud's candidacy was given a polemical aspect that he had not sought or probably foreseen. Conservative members of the Academy and others who decided to promote his case portrayed him as the anti-Zola, an author who opposed depicting man as a rutting beast constantly driven by his basest instincts.[3] That is an unfair characterization of Zola's body of work, though it is not an inaccurate description of certain parts of it. It is also an inaccurate characterization of Viaud's work up to this point. In *Iceland Fisherman* Viaud had reproduced some of the structure of Zola's novel about sometimes bestial coal miners, *Germinal* (1885), in order to offer a more positive presentation of France's working poor. (As Mary Dailey Desmarais has shown, structuring a work so as to recall another artist's creation and highlight the differences was a procedure practised by Monet as well.[4]) In *Madame Chrysanthemum* he had offered a positive presentation of Impressionist painting in part in response to Zola's condemnation of it the year before in *The Great Work of Art* (1886). Still, Viaud had written a fairly naturalist novel himself with *My*

Brother Yves and was not seeking a confrontation with Zola on personal or ideological grounds. His diary shows no feelings of rivalry with the naturalist at this time.

It took six rounds of voting for Loti to get a plurality. By that point Zola, who had had eight votes on the first ballot, received none. Press commentary on Viaud's election was generally favourable, though some of Zola's supporters were vehement in their denunciation of his victory.[5]

Viaud decided to use the very public platform of his reception speech – he knew it would appear in newspapers across France – to talk about his ideas on art, but also, only briefly, to distance himself from some of the naturalists. (He began work on his speech five months before he was scheduled to deliver it, so he did take it seriously.) The remarks he actually delivered at the Academy, on 7 April 1892, have been described as an attack on Zola, but they were not. All he said that afternoon about the naturalist novel was: 'after the remarkable masters of that school, into what indigestible pathos the mediocre practitioners of Naturalism who have followed them have fallen!' (*Speech*, 77). This was certainly an attack on some members of the 'school of Naturalism', as Zola liked to call it, a few of whom were little more than pretentious pornographers. Equally certainly, however, it was not an attack on their 'remarkable master'.

Viaud had originally intended to say more. The text that appeared in newspapers across France the next morning – sometimes on the front page, which shows how significant his election to the Academy had become – and which he published with Calmann-Lévy a few days later, is more than twice as long as the one he delivered at the Mazarin Palace. It contains further, harsher remarks regarding Naturalism, though again no ad hominem attacks on Zola. He describes naturalism as 'the excess' of realism, and continues:

I do not contest their rights. But, like great flames that rise from unclean straw, they have given off a thick and too invasive smoke. My condemnation of naturalism is that it finds its subjects uniquely in the dregs of the people found in the great cities that these authors prefer to inhabit. Never having looked elsewhere than that mud puddle, which is very particular and very limited, they go on to generalize without restraint in the observations they draw from those dregs. They therefore make outrageous mistakes. The people of the world they try to paint for us, the farmers, the labourers, all of them resembling the people you would meet in Belleville dance halls [then a working-class suburb of Paris], are completely false. The absolute vulgarity, the cynicism that makes fun of everything, are morbid phenomena unique to those lower-class Paris suburbs. I know this for a fact, coming as I do from the great open air outside the cities. This is why naturalism, as it is understood today, is destined – despite the monstrous talent of some of the writers in that school – to pass away, when the unhealthy curiosity that sustains it has worn itself out. (*Speech*, 49–51)

Despite Viaud's careful wording and praise for the 'remarkable masters' and their 'monstrous talent', Zola – who, unbeknown to Viaud, had been in the audience when he delivered his speech – took offence. (Zola was very defensive about his 'school', even though it included some second-rate authors.) The next day, perhaps after he had read the undelivered part of the text in the press, Zola granted an interview to a reporter from [the major Parisian daily] *Le Figaro* and remarked: 'It is customary, after a duel, for the fortunate adversary to avoid speaking of the man whom he wounded.' Zola described himself as 'wounded' but not dead, and suggested Viaud did not know how to behave as a gentleman. Viaud, who knew how to use the press as well as Zola (a former publicist), wrote a reply that was carried in various newspapers on

Loti in Academic regalia, 1892.

10 April. In it he assured his former dinner companion that if he had known the author was in the audience, he would have skipped the passage in his speech that referred to naturalism. He went on to add, however, that

> I find that you are mistaken, that you see men as they are not. And, what's more, you manage to make them be seen that way by the writers who walk in your wake [a strange metaphor for a seaman] and the thousands of readers who follow you.
>
> But that does not keep me from admiring your talent, believe me. It is general and immense. And if, yesterday, I bruised your feelings personally, I very much regret it.

Zola replied, again in the press, with reciprocal praise for Viaud's 'great and personal talent', but also remarked that he considered the writer to be 'one of us', a naturalist. He further suggested that Viaud had been tricked into attacking naturalism by unnamed others – that is, that he was naive enough to have allowed himself to be manipulated.[6]

There was truth in this quarrel on both sides. Even *Germinal*, which is a great, at times very powerful novel, becomes almost comical in its endless, puritanical preoccupation with the miners' often astounding sex drives. (Zola was married to a woman who evidently did not enjoy sex, at least as he wanted it. He definitely projected onto his miners his fantasies about what the working class must be enjoying unfettered by nineteenth-century bourgeois morality.) *The Earth*, which is not a great novel, goes to yet further extremes. Still, Viaud did repeatedly emphasize that he found fault not with Zola's work but with some of that written by his followers.

Zola was also right. Viaud's criticism that some of the naturalists depicted characters and types (farmers, labourers) who did not exist as presented outside a few working-class Paris suburbs meant that he accepted the precept that literature should strive to provide realistic, representative pictures of society, one of the tenets of French realism and naturalism, though one that Viaud had rejected in the climactic scene of *Madame Chrysanthemum*. And certainly *My Brother Yves* in some ways resembles naturalist fiction, especially its scenes of drunken labourers and their wives in Brest.

Both authors subsequently worked to repair the breach in their relationship. When his next novel, *La Débâcle*, a condemnation of Napoleon III and his failed war on Prussia, came out later in 1892, Zola sent Viaud a copy. Viaud replied with a letter of warm praise, condemning Zola's 'courtesans' for erecting a barrier between them. Subsequently they would continue to communicate. In 1920, eighteen years after Zola's early death and 28 after this incident, Viaud told his personal secretary, Gaston Mauberger, that Zola had paid him several visits when other chairs in the Academy became vacant, requesting Viaud's vote. 'He wasn't afraid of telling me: "The Academy would do itself honour by electing me." The Academy did not do itself honour, or rather, yes: it did itself honour by not admitting him!', Viaud told Mauberger.[7] Zola had a very high opinion of himself and did not hesitate to share it with the world, yes; but did Viaud really believe he did not deserve that often tarnished honour?

Goncourt, who saw himself as the (unacknowledged) father of naturalism, also took offence at Viaud's speech, though he even more clearly was not attacked in it. He wrote a coruscating denunciation of Viaud in his diary, claiming that whatever talent of observation and style was to be found in Viaud's work derived from those of Goncourt and his late brother Jules.[8] It is probably true that Viaud derived some of his more Impressionistic style from the Goncourt brothers' 'artistic prose', though the major influence there was Viaud's favourite author, Flaubert. Goncourt went back to having conversations with Viaud over dinner at Daudet's home a year or so after the younger man's election, however.

Viaud became more involved in the art world during this decade. He began to receive visits from painters of all sorts. Some passages in his diary written during his travels in this decade, such as a description of a landscape in Tunisia, have all the nuanced colour of an Impressionist canvas.

His circle of non-romantic female friends in this decade also continued to centre on the arts. First among them was Princess Alice of Monaco, whom he described in 1891 as 'the female friend I like/love the most' (*Journal III*, 355). He often saw her when he was in Paris. There she introduced him to another Impressionism-loving member of high society, Geneviève Straus, whose artist-filled weekly salon was already attended by the devoted and admiring young Marcel Proust. Her marriage to the wealthy banker Émile Straus, like Alice Heine's to the Duke of Richelieu, had brought her into a world that purchased a lot of contemporary art, including paintings by Claude Monet. Like the Princess, Straus brought with her a superior intelligence and quick wit, as well as an open mind, that captivated Viaud as it did Proust.[9] Sometimes the two women and Viaud went to the Opéra together.

One art-loving aristocrat Viaud saw less of during this decade was Queen Elisabeth of Romania. Because she had encouraged a romance between the heir to the Romanian throne and a Romanian aristocrat and poet, Elena Văcărescu, whom she had befriended as a sister spirit, Elisabeth was exiled from the kingdom for several years. She settled in Venice and there continued to write voluminously, inviting Viaud to visit. He did later in 1891. One of his diary remarks about her compositions, which she loved to read to him, suggests yet again that he was taking his art more seriously than ever: he accused her of 'disdaining the essential subsequent rewriting, which consists of tightening up one's thoughts, condensing and clarifying them for the reader' (*Journal III*, 385). These were not just facile words on his part. Henry James, who knew what it meant to devote serious time to reworking a text, wrote of Viaud's style near the end of this same decade: 'his particular shade of the natural was surely never arrived at without much choosing and comparing . . . But he covers his tracks, as I have hinted, consummately.'[10]

Another art-loving woman from whom Viaud became more distant during this last decade of the century was Juliette Adam. In late 1894 and early 1895 he allowed her to publish the first two parts of his lengthy description of his travels through the Holy Land, *Le Désert* (The Desert) and *Jérusalem* (Jerusalem). He gave the last part, *Galilée* (Galilee), to *Le Figaro*, however, and two of his best works from this decade, the novel *Ramuntcho* and the historical drama *Judith Renaudin*, to a new literary journal, *La Revue de Paris*. Between such 'infidelities' and a variety of political differences, plus the fact that Adam resented seeing her 'creation' taken under the protective wing of other influential women, the relationship between those two during this decade grew strained. As Alain Quella-Villéger has observed, Adam 'greatly feared competition in her friendships'.[11]

Less problematic was Viaud's relationship with Sarah Bernhardt, whom he continued to see regularly when he travelled to Paris. In August and September 1895, Viaud mentions in his diary that he is working 'feverishly' to finish a play for her which he refers to as *La Révocation de l'Édit de Nantes* (The Revocation of the Edict of Nantes), the 1685 act by which Louis XIV revoked protections previously accorded to Protestants (*Journal III*, 775–7). He reads it to her when she arrives in Rochefort on 6 September and she supposedly pronounces herself 'delighted' with it (*ravie*). Then there is silence until the following August, when, during another visit to Rochefort, she informs Viaud that she is still interested in the play. After that there is still more silence until Christmas Eve 1897, when Viaud announces that he has finished a drama about Judith Renaudin, one of his Protestant maternal ancestors who had suffered through Louis XIV's persecution of the Hugenots (*Journal IV, 174*). There is no mention of Sarah Bernhardt, however. On the other hand, in his 1931 memoirs of working with Viaud, theatre director André Antoine, who gave *Judith Renoudin* its world premiere at his Théâtre Antoine in 1898, recalls that, when he first met Viaud in November 1897, the author informed him that he had 'just found the substance [of his Huguenot drama *Judith Renaudin*] in some old family letters'.[12] Antoine produced the play without Bernhardt.

It is not too hard to imagine Viaud lying to Antoine about when he had started the play; he was not overly scrupulous about telling white lies. In the preface to the drama that he published with it in *La Revue de Paris* in November 1898, while the play was running at the Théâtre Antoine, Viaud declared that his family had preserved letters sent from Holland by Protestant ancestors who had fled France because of the Revocation, and that one of his grandmothers had occasionally read passages from them to him when he was young. Those letters, he continued, 'inspired me to write this drama' (*m'ont inspiré ce drame*).[13] This passage suggests that he had not 'just' come across the idea for the play before meeting Antoine for the first time in November 1897; indeed, it goes on to specify that 'the idea came to me to compose this play more than two years ago,' which would have been no later than 1896.[14] Equally importantly, Viaud's preface says only that the letters inspired him to write this drama, which is not the same as providing him with 'the substance' of the play. Nor could they have provided him with its substance. The real Judith Renaudin abjured her Huguenot faith in 1685 and did not go to Holland until around 1700, and then evidently for commercial rather than religious reasons, unlike her namesake in the play. Viaud may not have wanted Antoine to know that the play had originally been written for someone else, though it is hard to understand why, unless Bernhardt finally rejected it for some reason. He may have wanted Antoine to believe the play recounted a true story, which it does not. It is also possible that, thirty-plus years after the event, Antoine misremembered Viaud's exact wording at their initial meeting.

More importantly, however, it is definitely hard to imagine Viaud having written the play Antoine produced in 1898 and which we have today for Bernhardt at that point in her career. By the mid-1890s the great tragedienne was famous for appearing in lavishly staged costume dramas about powerful queens and other larger-than-life historical figures. (She did, in fact, continue to appear occasionally in a greater variety of roles, even as peasant women, on tour, especially outside France. In Paris, however, she kept to her costumed spectaculars because, as she told an admirer, 'they wanted to see her in beautiful dresses.'[15]) To judge from contemporary reports and the few recordings she made, Bernhardt evidently performed those roles in a highly dramatic manner, full of sighs and sobs. Judith Renaudin is the simple, obedient but independent daughter of a modest Protestant family who refuses to give in to pressure to convert or to marry, preferring rather to leave her beloved elderly relatives and go into exile unmarried. That is not the sort of role Bernhardt was playing at this point in her career. She had made a speciality of women torn apart by carnal desire they could not control, modern versions of her great classical theatre triumph, Jean Racine's *Phèdre*. Judith Renaudin is in love with no man and experiences no such desires.

Viaud evidently penned something dealing with the Revocation of the Edict of Nantes for Bernhardt in 1895. When she, for whatever reason, did not subsequently perform it, he must have altered what he had to create the work that Antoine staged in November 1898. The fact that, in his diary entry describing Bernhardt at the dress rehearsal on 2 November of that year, Viaud makes no mention of having originally created the play for her suggests that what they watched that afternoon was not what he had written for, and read to, her three years before.[16]

Judith Renaudin deserves to be better known. It uses a famous event in seventeenth-century France to comment on a dramatic moment in modern history. Oscar Wilde – whom

Bernhardt knew, having hoped to perform his play *Salomé* in London during her 1892 season there – had been imprisoned for sodomy in May 1895, a case that received much, often negative, press coverage in France.[17] His wife forced him to give up his parental rights to their two young sons and he never saw them again. Upon release in May 1897, Wilde promptly moved to France to escape England's laws against homosexual activity, inciting more negative French press commentary. As J. E. Rivers has written, 'the Wilde affair cast a pall of paranoia over the subject of homosexuality [in France].'[18]

Viaud, himself the father of two young sons by November 1895, the second a child conceived with his Basque mistress, of whom more shortly, had been rumoured to be homosexual in the French press ever since the publication of *My Brother Yves* in 1883. Various memoirs from the end of the nineteenth century show that speculation about his sexual proclivities was common, not just in the yellow press but in some of the worlds he frequented. One evening in May 1888, for example, at the Parisian salon of Countess Diane de Beausacq, one of Viaud's staunchest supporters, a new guest observed that the Countess and the author Jean Aicard, a friend of Viaud's, had to defend the writer's reputation because 'of course, everyone says bad things about him [*tout le monde dit du mal à son propos*] . . . People reproach him for a defect that is a matter of bad luck, the worst luck in the world.'[19] Viaud already did enough other things when in society to make himself the butt of ridicule, such as wearing built-up heels and leaning forward on his toes to compensate for his short stature. He must have been accustomed to, if not happy with, a lot of half-hidden snickering when he entered a room. After reading a mocking attack on him in the press, he had confessed in an unguarded moment: 'If I am really like that, at least up until now I have been in the company of people charitable enough and with enough taste not to let me know it.'[20]

Nevertheless Viaud and Antoine cast the openly gay 29-year-old actor Edouard de Max as Judith's father, Samuel Renaudin. De Max was known for and accustomed to playing characters his own age, such as Racine's Nero in *Britannicus*, a work in which he also starred in 1898. Samuel Renaudin is described in the play as 'almost an old man', however, and spends most of his time onstage worrying that he will lose his children because he belongs to a persecuted minority, the Huguenots. This against-the-grain casting must have raised eyebrows and made audiences wonder what Antoine was up to. De Max had known Wilde from the latter's previous stay in Paris in 1891 and had starred in the Paris premiere of *Salomé* at the Théâtre de l'Oeuvre in 1896, so he was associated with the disgraced Irish poet. The rest of the play centres not around religious issues but rather various characters' efforts to force Samuel's daughter, Judith, to marry, which she, like Viaud, does not want to do.

Given all this, it is not hard to see how Viaud could have invented this story – all the while claiming, disingenuously, that it had been inspired by his maternal family history – as a way of expressing anxiety over growing homophobia in France and how it might affect his relationship with his first son, especially given his poor relationship with his wife.[21] This would explain why the person he invited to join Bernhardt and himself for the dress rehearsal was Robert de Montesquiou, a minor poet and aristocratic aesthete who, unlike Viaud, made little effort to hide his homosexual proclivities and was ridiculed in the press for them. (Montesquiou was supposedly Huysmans's model for des Esseintes in *Against the Grain* and at least one of Proust's models for the Baron de Charlus in *In Search of Lost Time*.) Viaud had been raised with stories of the persecution of his Protestant ancestors. With the Wilde trial and the reaction to it in France, it would not have been hard for him to see the current persecution of another minority to which he appeared to belong in terms of the one he had grown up hearing about. Choosing de Max, an openly gay actor who customarily played young leads, to portray the elderly Samuel Renaudin may have been Viaud's way of signalling to at least part of the audience that it should wonder why the role had been cast in so unusual a manner.

Wilde was in Paris in November 1898, when the drama was performed. He had seen Antoine's production of Hauptmann's *Die Weber* (The Weavers) six months before, but there is no indication in his correspondence whether he saw *Judith Renaudin*.

Also in this decade things come to a sad end with Pierre Le Cor, who evidently did not enjoy being seen by the literature-reading world as Viaud's homosexually complacent 'brother Yves'. He continued to deal with alcoholism, getting in trouble because of it. Viaud helped him out, informing his diary that 'I have so detached myself from him that I do it out of duty, with complete indifference' (*Journal III*, 379). Nevertheless, an entry from 11 September 1918, in the logbook of Viaud's personal secretary, Gaston Mauberger, shows that Viaud was sending Le Cor and his wife a monthly 'pension' even then.[22]

Chief among the men in Viaud's life during this decade was still Léo Thémèze, he of the 'godlike' younger beauty. The fact that Thémèze at one point gets married doesn't seem to put a hitch in this, as it had not with Le Cor previously except in the novelization of that relationship. In 1893 Viaud confides to his diary that Thémèze is

> still the one whose soul I feel to be the closest to mine
> and the most similar. The true brother, who under-
> stands me to my depths, and whom I would like to
> have near me in the hour of death. (*Journal III*, 534)

Viaud's comment that Léo 'understood him to his depths', as he had claimed Le Cor and other 'brothers' had done in the past, may indicate, as much as anything else, that Viaud found in these very masculine men an acceptance of him as he wanted to be seen with whatever explanations for his behaviour he wanted others to believe. Being accepted by men, 'real men', was very important to Viaud. Thémèze, like Le Cor before him, was a 'real man' who was evidently willing to accept Viaud as he was without ridicule. That, along with his great physical beauty, seems to have made him very attractive to the author.

In 1892 Viaud wrote a novel, *Matelot* (translated into English as 'Jean Berny, Sailor'), whose main character is based on Thémèze. Unlike *My Brother Yves*, it does not deal with another man's love for him. It is the least memorable of Viaud's novels and did not sell well. In 1897 Thémèze wrote to him: 'I can figure you out but I cannot say who you are . . . your depths remain mysterious.'[23] When Viaud decided to visit the Holy Land in 1894, he took Thémèze along as his companion. On the way back, they stopped in Constantinople, where Viaud found it strange to be with Léo in places he recalled from his days with Mehmet almost twenty years before.

Why did Viaud undertake this trip to the Holy Land? He was, as he stated more than once, 'of all men the most unbelieving', and that did not change as a result of this expedition (*Journal III*, 398). While salvation from sin did not interest this lapsed Protestant, he was concerned with finding some assurance that he would be united with his deceased loved ones somewhere after his own death. His travels through the Holy Lands did not provide him with that.

They did, however, allow him to go back to consideration of the functions of art. On 20 April, for example, while he and Léo are in Galilee near Nazareth, he gazes out over the fields and hills and decides that what he is viewing must have looked and sounded the same 1,900 years before, when Jesus regularly walked that same ground. When he returns to France and expands this passage of the diary in the third volume of his travel narrative

Galilee, he extrapolates artistic consequences from it. 'Often in his evening reveries [Jesus] must have stopped here, on these heights overlooking this isolated town, and contemplated these same horizons, let his gaze wander for a long time over these same aspects,' he supposes (*Galilee*, Ch. 4). Perhaps, Viaud then speculates, when he faced death on Golgotha, Jesus thought back on these same peaceful horizons. While we cannot know Jesus's feelings for particular individuals, Viaud decides, can we not, by gazing carefully at what he saw every day, come to know at least part of his thoughts and feelings? And so:

> On Gethsemane, on Golgotha, when the hour of fear came when everything in him that was human grew anguished at the idea of the approaching annihilation [no notion of afterlife here], perhaps he saw once again, in his last dreams – as the least of us would have done – the mountains familiar to him from his childhood, the sad gulf of grasses along the edge of the plain of Esdrelon, and the tranquil grazing lands up above where, during the evening then as now, were heard the shepherds' calls to their goats on their pipes – in short, all the things that we are looking at there in front of us . . . similar to what they must have been two thousand years ago. (*Galilee*, Ch. 4)

This reflects the Romantic belief that we are what we feel as much as, if not more than, what we think, a philosophical position in line with both Viaud's and Monet's way of viewing themselves, as we have seen. Moreover, Viaud suggests that, in areas of the world that have not changed physically in a long time, we should be able to understand how even ancient inhabitants thought and, more importantly, felt by contemplating the same natural sights that they were in the habit of viewing, since our natural surroundings shape, to at least an extent, our emotions though our vision of them. (Viaud had not proposed this when he was in the parts of Brittany that he believed to have remained unchanged since prehistoric, or at least Gallo-Roman, times.) As Viaud intimates several times in his Holy Land narrative, and then more clearly in the major novel that followed it, *Ramuntcho* (1897), of which more shortly, this meant that a good painter – even if with words – who could show us what previous men saw could, if he depicted such scenes effectively, allow his reader-viewers to experience those previous inhabitants' thoughts and feelings as well. Painting for Viaud was no longer 'just' a way of communicating his own feelings to his reader-viewers, therefore – Monet's and Marie Viaud's 'what I feel'. Done properly, it could, he now believed, become a medium by which the artist allowed his reader-viewers to share the emotions of others across both time and space – share them in an immediate way. The eccentric who was transforming his house into a collection of time- and space-travel machines had come to understand that, through carefully crafted works of art, he could provide similar cross-cultural voyages of understanding to his reader-viewers wherever they read or 'viewed' his books.

This is an understanding to which Viaud held firm. Fifteen years later, when he was transforming his notes on a visit to Angkor Wat in Cambodia into a travel narrative, he wrote in the last chapter that 'most men [are] simple playthings of their initial impressions. Little nothings, looked at for a long time when one is very young, are all it takes to bend all the rest of one's destiny one way or the other.'[24]

This realization during his travels through the Holy Land may explain why, soon after he returned to Rochefort, Viaud set about transforming his diary pages from the trip into a three-volume narrative. It is by far the longest he ever wrote, through the travels themselves covered only a few months and were no longer than some of his other trips. This shows that the author was continuing the time-consuming artistic crafting that he had practised in his previous art texts. The three volumes are painterly as *To Morocco* had been painterly, with little action and much often carefully honed description. Three volumes of that does not make for exciting reading, true, but if you are in the right mood, some of it can be very enjoyable.

The last major event in Viaud's life during this decade involved both another exotic land and another person, or persons, but in this case it was much closer to home and there was virtually no love involved. It did, however, involve his career as a naval officer, to which we need to return.

Ever since Viaud published his article on the front page of *Le Figaro* in 1883 describing the massacre of Indochinese civilians by French troops, the French navy had done its best to assign him to posts that would keep him out of trouble. They couldn't stop him from publishing, though he was supposed to get approval on everything he published; but they could distance him from regions where French colonial policy was provoking the most controversy at home and abroad.

Few locations met that criterion better than the southwest corner of France along the Spanish border, in the Basque country. There the biggest problem was stopping Basques who saw themselves as neither French nor Spanish from running contraband over a border that meant little to them. Since Viaud had no interest in career advancement by then and since, as his mother got older, he preferred to be stationed near her, this assignment worked well for him. He was appointed commander of the *Javelot*, a gunboat that patrolled the Bidassoa, the river forming the border between France and Spain that flows into the Atlantic. With the exception of an office assignment in Rochefort from June 1893 to May 1896, Viaud commanded the *Javelot* from December 1891 to January 1898.

This Basque assignment led to Viaud's last major achievement as a novelist. He could have remained on the Basque coast, as most tourists to the region do even today, in the seaside resorts like

Biarritz and Saint-Jean-de-Luz made fashionable by the Empress Eugénie during the Second Empire. Just as he had not been content with that when he was stationed in Constantinople and Brittany almost two decades before, however, so it did not suffice for him in the 1890s. Instead, he made friends with Basque sailors under his command, went inland with them to visit their towns and families, and so discovered a people who, like the Bretons, had their own language and culture – one that, like the Breton, was not only very different from that of nineteenth-century France but also, at least to Viaud, much older, much closer to the origins of mankind. In fact, the Basque region became his new Brittany, with – for him – many of the features that had fascinated him in Brittany decades before.

By October 1892, he is telling his diary that he finds the Basque language, which is related to no other, 'mysterious and *sauvage* [wild, uncultivated]', the second adjective one that he had often applied to Brittany, especially its interior (*Journal III*, 461). The people who spoke it, he was delighted to discover, descended from unknown but evidently very ancient origins. When he travelled inland with his Basque friend Joseph Brahy, yet another handsome sailor and Viaud's aide-de-camp, to visit Brahy's birthplace, Viaud described the excursion in a way reminiscent of the journey he took to Saint-Pol-de-Léon thirteen years before with Pierre Le Cor when that sailor decided to find his own origins. When Viaud subsequently transformed those diary pages into Part I, Chapters Fifteen and Sixteen of *Ramuntcho*, the trip undertaken by the title character and his friend Arrochkoa to Erribiague, deep inside the Basque region, to discover information about Arrochkoa's father, goes well beyond Chapters Nine and Ten in *My Brother Yves*. The deeper the two young Basques penetrate into the interior, the wilder and more *sauvage* Arrochkoa becomes.[25] Unlike in *My Brother Yves*, Viaud was now suggesting that modern, supposedly civilized man could revert to his prehistoric origins if he renewed contact with them, something that he could have argued for Yves Kermadec, for example, but never did after Kermadec's first appearance in *Blossoms of Boredom*. Also unlike in *My Brother Yves* or other of Viaud's works dealing with the prehistoric elements of Brittany, in *Ramuntcho* the author presents those primitive forces as potentially very dangerous. It is understandable why Joseph Conrad made such extensive use of the novel when he wrote *Heart of Darkness*.[26]

Nonetheless, Viaud became very involved in Basque culture, learning to play *pelote*, the fast-paced ball game, and even going on contraband outings at night, he whose job during the day was, in part, to prevent them. As in the past, Viaud was not trying to become someone else. Rather, by integrating himself into aspects of Basque culture, he found ways of creating yet another of the diverse characters who comprised Pierre Loti. In 1894 he even bought a house in Hendaye, on the border between Spain and France.

As he had in Brittany, so in the Basque region Viaud came to see the people as possessing a life force, a strength that, for all his gymnastics and continued physical training, he felt that he lacked. This is in part why, when he decided that his son was growing up to be his wife's child more than his, he started to contemplate fathering a second set of sons, this time with a Basque mother who would instill in them some of that vital force he found lacking in the often sickly Samuel. In 1893, by which time the boy was four, Viaud told his diary that 'my son Samuel seems more than ever like a *little de Ferrière* . . . all this ties me even more to the time when I was thinking more than ever of escaping altogether, of creating a family for myself elsewhere' (*Journal III*, 531).

As a result, he sets out to find a healthy Basque woman who can provide him with such sons. He settles on Crucita Gainza, the 26-year-old sister of his Basque *pelote* and contraband partner Ramoncho Gainza. (Viaud was 43 by then.) He meets her in October 1893. 'I can't say that I feel a great attraction for her,' he confessed to his diary two months later. 'It's rather a question of trust and affection, which is better, because I am taking her above

Notice in the Rochefort newspaper of Raymond Gainza's birth, 30 June 1895.

all else to be the mother of my children' (*Journal III*, 578). The next spring he sets off for the Holy Land, putting their 'strange marriage', as he terms it, on hold until his return (*Journal III*, 579).

In fact, there was never any question of a real marriage. Viaud had no intention of divorcing Blanche, with whom he had developed a relationship that worked well for him. Crucita would become little more than an incubator and wet nurse for his 'primitive' progeny. Her piety and frequent trips to church, Catholic church, lead Viaud to conclude that 'I believe she will simply be what I wanted her to be: a healthy mother for my children' (*Journal III*, 728). Several months in the Holy Land had not made Viaud any more tolerant of religious zeal than he had been before he left. By 20 October 1894, Viaud is delighted to report that Crucita is already pregnant: 'I hardly dare to believe that my desire has been fulfilled so quickly' (*Journal III*, 734).

Initially he set up the pregnant Crucita in a household in Rochefort, walking distance from his – and his wife's – own. Rochefort was not that big, and as Viaud knew from the days when his father stole money from city hall and his family lost their home, malicious gossip travelled fast. Men with a mission can be blind to everything else, but it is hard to imagine that Viaud could have thought his legitimate family would not discover what was going on almost literally under their noses. Julien and Crucita's first child, named Ramoncho (Raymond in French) after his uncle, was born on 29 June 1895. The next day there was a notice in the Rochefort newspaper: he is listed simply as Raymond, with no last name. Viaud would never legally recognize him or his two brothers. If they were to continue him in this world after his death, they would not continue his name.

Even if he did not legally recognize him, Viaud was proud of this new son, proud enough to show him off, which he had not done with Samuel. One of the first persons he took to see the baby was Léo, in early September. Far more surprising is that at the end of 1895, while Blanche and Samuel were in Bordeaux, Viaud had the child brought to his home and, after first showing him to his niece, Marie's daughter Ninette, led the little child to meet his 85-year-old mother. Only after Nadine Viaud embraced the baby and he was carried away did Viaud tell her whom she had just kissed. 'She trembles all over, profoundly moved [*émue*] by this revelation until evening,' he told his diary (*Journal III*, 803).

Crucita shortly thereafter moves back to her homeland. It is easy to understand why. She was isolated in Rochefort, cut off from her family – who were not happy about what she had done – and probably not able to communicate with anyone, since she does not appear to have known much French. This creates something of a problem for Viaud as well, because when he subsequently visits his son he can only communicate with gestures and smiles. And yet, Raymond was very important to him, as were Alphonse Lucien, called Edmond, born in 1897, and Charles Fernand, who died within his first year. In the end, the idea of a second family seems to have failed him, though. Already by 4 September 1900, Viaud is confessing to his diary that his Basque sons 'have not taken the place I hoped for in my life' (*Journal IV*, 438).

There was nothing exceptional about a nineteenth-century married French bourgeois having a mistress. In a country that had only allowed divorce again in 1884, it was common and even in certain circles a sign of financial success. Remember *Gigi*. It was less common, certainly, for a man to want to have children by his mistress, but that was not unheard of either, especially if, for whatever reason, he could not have them with his legitimate spouse. Zola was reportedly delighted that his mistress, Jeanne Rozerot, presented him with two children, since his wife Alexandrine could not. What is unusual is that Viaud seems to have chosen his mistress almost uniquely for her child-bearing qualities. He did not find her attractive and did not approve of or support her religious devotion. When she insisted that Ramoncho be baptized in a Catholic church, for example, Viaud refused to attend.

Dealing with such a mistress clearly played a part in the development of *Ramuntcho*, the novel Viaud wrote about the Basques during this decade. It is one of his major works, indeed a major work of late nineteenth-century French fiction, so it is worth devoting some time to it, especially since it is too often dismissed as a simple sentimental novel about young love. It does contain a story about fairly innocent lovers. To dismiss it as nothing more than that, however, is not wise.

The novel tells the story of a young man, Ramuntcho, the son of a cultured, sophisticated French painter and a simple, uneducated

Basque woman – basically, Viaud's relationship with Crucita, but also, in various ways, his relationships with Pierre Le Cor, Léo Thémèze and some of his other 'brothers' after Joseph Bernard. Ramuntcho wants to be accepted by his fellow Basques, which he attempts to bring about by smuggling and playing *pelote* with them, just as Viaud did while stationed in the Basque area. At the same time, however, and especially after having been away for his two years of military service in France, the young man has problems accepting a culture in which everyone does the same thing in the same unthinking way, symbolized by the (male) audience at the *pelote* matches, all of whom wear their berets – then seen as very Basque, not yet Parisian – in the same fashion. The young man dreams of leaving this closed, conforming world for South America with his girlfriend, Gracieuse, to make a living playing *pelote*. He loses her to a convent when she falls under the spell of the Catholic Church, however, not unlike Crucita. His mother also tries to keep him near her, not unlike Viaud's own mother Nadine. Ramuntcho's curious young mind is awakened by many things, first among them books. The more he thinks for himself, however, the more he becomes aware of all the forces around him that are trying to control him and his thought, much like Judith Renaudin.

This was more than a personal issue. Once the Third Republic settled into power in the late 1870s, it began a wide-ranging secularization of French government and culture, including the establishment of free public education in 1886. The Catholic Church and its adherents in France reacted to this strongly. (One of the better-known outgrowths of their reaction was the construction of Sacré-Coeur basilica in Montmartre.) By the 1890s, some republicans feared that France might slip back under the control of the Catholic Church. Émile Zola, for example, castigated mindless religious belief in his novel *Lourdes*, a copy of which he sent Viaud in July 1894, just after the latter's return from the Holy Land – which could have looked ominous to the anti-clerical Zola – at which point Viaud was probably setting back to work on *Ramuntcho*.

Throughout *Ramuntcho*, one sombre landscape description after the next shows night and shadow emerging from the always hovering Gizune mountain. (The real mountain on which the Gizune was based, the Rhune, is not much more than a tall hill.) These sometimes very beautiful descriptive passages evoke painting, but not Impressionism. Rather, they summon to mind Rembrandt's few, equally menacing landscapes, and not without reason. As Alison McQueen has shown, liberal, anti-establishment nineteenth-century French art critics and historians seized on the Dutch artist, who had not previously been admired as much as some of his contemporaries, and developed around him a myth that transformed him into 'the favored model for non-conformist and anti-establishment aims'.[27] Liberal historians and art historians took to presenting Rembrandt as having 'embodied the anti-Catholic . . . sentiments they wanted to promote in their own country'.[28] As McQueen observes, 'French critics and writers [at the end of the nineteenth century] believed Rembrandt's art, like Luther's doctrine, was a driving force behind the rejection of Catholicism in the Netherlands and the evolving Dutch democracy.'[29] Viaud knew Rembrandt's work and had cited it as justification for his own way of writing.[30] Putting *Ramuntcho* in this art-historical context lets us see why this time the author chose to evoke the Dutch master's landscapes in his novel about the threat of unthinking devotion to the survival of free minds.[31]

Perhaps because of the beauty of those descriptions, perhaps because of its theme of intellectual freedom and the dark forces that threatened it, *Ramuntcho* quickly proved to be one of Viaud's most popular books. Today it is the most often encountered in France after *Iceland Fisherman*, and deservedly so. Evidently in part because of his experiences in the Basque region, Viaud had come to realize that he could use his art in a freedom fight in his own day similar to the one that liberal republican historians were attributing to his Dutch predecessor. The novel's end is not a cinematic scene of triumph, which may disappoint some American readers. If they put the book down and look at the world around them, however, they will observe that, more than a century after its publication, Ramuntcho's, Viaud's and Zola's struggle to combat the forces that threaten free minds has yet to be won. As with *Judith Renaudin* in 1898, Viaud's focus in *Ramuntcho* was freedom of thought and personal choice.

In November 1899, he set off for India, this time taking the 'athletic, proudly handsome' Edmond Gueffier along as a companion (*Journal IV*, 284). The French Academy had charged him with delivering a decoration to the Maharajah of Travancore. The fact was, however, that Viaud wanted to meet with spiritual leaders there, including the English theosophist Annie Besant, about issues he was reticent to put into print, apparently because he feared being mocked for them. For some time after this trip he seems to have felt a real detachment from the things in his life, which is one of the teachings he learned there. On the way back, he rode through what was then Persia, visiting some of the remarkable ruins and, as he had done in India, taking some atmospheric photographs.[32] He would later develop his diary entries for this trip into two separate travel narratives, *L'Inde (sans les Anglais)* (India [without the English, 1903]), and *Vers Ispahan* (To Ispahan, 1904), the latter the only Viaud travel narrative not available in English – an unfortunate omission.

9

A Feminist in Spite of Himself? (1900–1906)

In 1898, arguing that France needed to rejuvenate its officer corps, the Minister of the Navy announced forced retirement for 28 older officers who were no longer serving in the fighting fleet. At the head of the list was the 48-year-old lieutenant Julien Viaud. His lack of ambition and efforts to remain close to his ageing mother – and his myriad romantic interests – had finally caught up with him. Viaud felt that there was animosity towards him in the naval hierarchy, and he was probably right. Nevertheless, he liked being in the navy when it suited him and got along well with the men who served with and under him. So, thanks to help from Juliette Adam, with whom he had smoothed over the strains in their relationship, he managed to get himself reinstated somewhat over a year later.

To prove his commitment, he allowed himself to be assigned to the fleet that was being sent to China along with ships from seven other powers to put down the Boxer Rebellion, a nationalist reaction to increased Western encroachment in that country. As his aide-de-camp he took a 25-year-old Frenchman with the misleadingly Turkish name of Osman Daney.

The *Redoutable*, on which Viaud and Daney were to sail, was waiting in Cherbourg. The author arrived there two days before departure and, wandering the streets at night, recorded experiencing 'a thousand difficult or sad memories that lay in wait to jump out at me in every part of this city' (*Journal IV*, 431). The diary editors, Quella-Villéger and Vercier, suggest that this refers

Loti, *c.* 1900, a frigate captain and an Officer of the Legion of Honour.

to the time he spent there in June 1873, with Joseph Bernard, and it might. It may also refer to the times he was there as 'madame' to Pierre Le Cor's 'monsieur' in 1882. Viaud had managed to compile a complicated sentimental history.

The *Redoutable* arrived in China in September 1900, by which time most of the rebellion had been suppressed. The Boxers had committed atrocities against Westerners and Christians. Viaud recorded examples in his diary that do not constitute easy reading. Western troops also committed atrocities, however, in addition to wide-scale pillage. Viaud recorded and commented on that as well. He saw 'an astonishing confusion of soldiers from the seven allied nations searching, marauding, destroying. The great barbarian invasions [of Europe during the Middle Ages] must have resembled this' (*Journal IV*, 442–3).

The published text Viaud derived from those diary pages, *Les Derniers Jours de Pékin*, translated into English keeping the original title as *The Last Days of Peking*, did not begin serialization until the next year. It appeared not in a literary-political journal like *La Revue des deux mondes* or *La Nouvelle Revue*, but in the newspaper *Le Figaro*, perhaps because it dealt with events that had been in the headlines. Having just fought to get reinstated in the service, Viaud did not want to risk a repetition of what had happened when he published his article on the French war in Indochina in 1883. Rather than submitting his report from the front as he had done then, he spent months reworking it while he was in Asia. In the process, he removed observations and descriptions critical of the French forces.

In addition, and to an even greater degree than in the three travel narratives he had derived from his trip to the Holy Land the decade before, Viaud polished his original text. As he had made clear with the first of his travel books, *To Morocco*, in 1889, he took these narratives very seriously as works of art, just as he had most of his last novels.

Unlike with those novels, however, this artistry posed something of a problem. Whereas readers are not surprised to encounter artistry in a novel, they expect anecdotal 'truth' in a travel narrative. Authors of the latter are not supposed to invent things; they are supposed to report what they saw and experienced. Viaud did that to an extent, certainly. But even in *To Morocco*, which is based on only about thirty pages of diary, some of the events and especially the descriptions may have been products of the author's painterly imagination as much as his memory. 'It's true, I embellish, and not just characters, settings [*décors*] as well,' Viaud told journalist Jean Joseph-Renaud. 'That is very much my literary right. Rembrandt and Veronese did not paint their Dutch or Venetian models with rigorous exactitude. Limiting oneself to copying is not an artistic obligation for a writer.'[1] This was something Viaud generally kept to himself, however.

Once again, there is a parallel in Monet's work at this time. That artist had made a great to-do in the press and among his professional acquaintances about his *plein-air* (out in nature) way of painting. He worked in front of the motif, he was always announcing, no matter how difficult that was. Unlike the Academic painters of his day, he did not paint in a studio.

This was largely true early in his career. The canvas that gave its name to the Impressionist movement, Monet's *Impression: Sunrise* (1872), for example, may well have been done in one session while the artist was standing at the port of Le Havre. As time went on, however, Monet became more and more intent on crafting his canvases to highlight the wealth of visual experience he found in a fleeting impression and his emotional reaction to it. He told the American painter Theodore Robinson that he worked a lot on some of his later paintings because he hoped that the buyer would therefore be able to 'live for longer with one of these canvases', find more in them of interest.[2] In order to accomplish this, he spent more and more time back in the studio honing paintings that he – still – began in front of the motif. As Monet scholar John House observed: 'Monet valued both [the appearance of] spontaneity and finish, and struggled to reconcile their conflicting claims.'[3] He also came to find easy subjects boring. 'As he was starting the Grain Stacks series in 1890, he told [Gustave] Geffroy that "more than ever easy things which come at one go disgust me."'[4] By the time he got to his series paintings, first those done on Belle-Île-en-Mer in Brittany in 1886, and then the famous *Haystacks*, *Poplars* and

Rouen Cathedral series from the 1890s that cemented his standing as France's greatest living painter, Monet was doing more and more honing back in his studio – though denying this when confronted with the facts.[5]

Viaud did much the same thing with his travel narratives. His preface to *The Last Days of Peking*, a dedication to the commander of the French fleet in the Boxer Rebellion expedition, Vice-Admiral Edouard Pottier, begins:

> the notes that I sent from China to *Le Figaro* will be gathered together in a volume that will be published in Paris before my return there, without it being possible for me to go over them. I am therefore rather worried about what such a collection might be. . . You will be indulgent with this book more than any other person because you know in what conditions it was written, day by day, during our difficult campaign, amid the continual agitation of our life on board ship. (*Peking*, Dedication)

It is true that Viaud was not able to rework the serialized version of *The Last Days of Peking* for its book-form publication. That serialized version was far from the diary entries that he had recorded in China 'day by day', however. In a subsequent paragraph of the dedication Viaud went on to describe the French troops in China as 'good and almost brotherly towards the most humble Chinese', clearly an attempt to show that he was not about to repeat the denunciation of French soldiers run wild that had got him into so much trouble in Indochina.

Viaud continued this approach to his travel narratives, which were now the main focus of his creative writing, for the rest of this decade. Back in Rochefort, he spent much of 1902–3 transforming his diary notes from his trip to Asia into *India* and *Toward Ispahan*. Both, but especially *Toward Ispahan*, show Viaud the painter with words intent on creating verbal canvases.[6]

The war in China was largely adjourned during the winter of 1900–1901, so the *Redoutable* was sent for repair and R&R to Nagasaki until April 1901. Then, after a final month in China, it returned to Japan until October, resulting in a longer stay there than Viaud had experienced in 1885. The author enjoyed this time in Japan more than he had fifteen years before. Perhaps it was the contrast with the horrors of China, but he told his diary that he found it amusing how 'at home' he felt on the island (*Journal IV*, 580). These diary pages, too, again with a great deal of artistry, Viaud transformed several years later into something between a travel narrative and a pleasant, non-erotic romance: *La Troisième Jeunesse de Madame Prune* (The Third Youth of Madame Prune, 1905). It is less a sequel to *Madame Chrysanthemum*, though it does revisit some of the same characters, than an idyll among the cherry blossoms.

When the *Redoutable* arrived at Saigon (today Ho Chi Minh City) on the voyage back to France, Viaud was able to get away for a month to visit a site that had fascinated him since he was a boy: the ruins of Angkor, the ancient Khmer capital of Cambodia. The French explorer Henri Mouhot had described them, with drawings, in diaries that were published in 1863–4. Viaud was thirteen at the time and, if we are to believe *The Story of a Child*, already dreaming of travels to exotic parts of the world because of just such illustrated publications. His description of sailing up the Mekong river is reminiscent of Ramuntcho and Arrochkoa's trip into the dark heart of the Basque country, a voyage back in time to an era of primitive origins from which Conrad borrowed in *Heart of Darkness*. Once again, Viaud took his time transforming these diary notes into a book, *Un Pèlerin d'Angkor* (A Pilgrimage to Angkor, 1912), one of his most beautifully evocative travel narratives, on which he did not start work for almost a decade. For the first time since *To Morocco*, the pre-publication serialization, again in *L'Illustration*, included illustrations, though this time photographs rather than artwork.

Viaud was intent on making his readers see what he described, this time without the interference of another artist.[7]

When he finally arrived back in Rochefort in April 1902, Viaud felt that not much had changed. He remained disappointed with Samuel, finding him 'frail' and 'lacking the physical qualities that I wanted him to have' (*Journal IV*, 644). On the other hand, Raymond and Edmond, his two Basque sons, were 'cute, funny, vigorous', the last in particular the quality he had hoped to import from the older, more 'primitive' Basque race (*Journal IV*, 645).

He saw some of his art-loving friends in Paris, though they now also made the trip to Rochefort to visit him. When Princess Alice of Monaco, about to separate from the Prince because of her infidelities, makes that trip, he introduces her to Raymond and Edmond. When Sarah Bernhardt travels to see him in March 1903, it is to commission another play, this time a collaborative effort with Judith Gautier that eventually becomes *La Fille du ciel* (The Daughter of Heaven).

As with *Judith Renaudin* – of which there is no mention in Viaud's diary when he writes of this new commission – Bernhardt's intentions with respect to this play remain difficult to reconstruct. The daughter of poet Théophile Gautier, Judith (1845–1917) was herself a writer of distinction, becoming the first woman member of the Académie Goncourt in 1910. From her attendance at her father's *salon* she grew up knowing some of the major writers of the day, including the Goncourt brothers and Flaubert. Her father gave her a Chinese tutor, so she learned the language and spent much of the rest of her life writing on Chinese themes. In the end, it was Gautier who actually wrote the play, turning it over act by act to Viaud so that he could make a few minor adjustments and give it his imprimatur.[8] On 1 May 1904, *Le Figaro* announced that '*The Daughter of Heaven*, the great Chinese drama in six tableaux commissioned by Mme Sarah Bernhardt from Mme Judith Gautier and M Pierre Loti, was turned over yesterday to the great artist for whom it was written, and who will perform it next season.'[9] In fact, she never performed it – though, unlike with *Judith Renaudin*, it is easy to imagine her in the title role.

The Daughter of Heaven was not staged until 1912, when it received a spectacular production at the new Century Theater in New York City. Viaud, who travelled to New York for the opening, was overwhelmed by both the production and his reception. In an article he published in French the following year in the New York City magazine *The Century*, he declared that 'no Parisian theatre would have risked' such elaborate sets, or have known how to bring off such startling lighting effects. 'Thanks to the conscientious magic of the set painters and costume designers, old imperial China . . . is there before me.'[10] The reviews were only fair, praising the production but not the play itself. It ran for a respectable 98 performances and then disappeared.[11]

Viaud also served as play doctor for his friend Émile Vedel's translation of *King Lear*. Antoine produced it at his Théâtre Antoine on 30 November 1904. It was, for once, a real triumph, enough so that Antoine revived it for several years. It was Viaud's only real theatrical success, though, as he told theatre director Jules Claretie, he had only a small role in its creation. He also adapted *Ramuntcho* for the stage, but like his dramatization of *Iceland Fisherman* it was not a lasting success. *Judith Renaudin* remains by far his best original achievement in drama. Even it, though interesting, is not great theatre.

Viaud also resumed his love life. There were the usual passionate encounters with unnamed women. Léo Thémèze, by this time an officer in the merchant marine, realized that he no longer occupied first place in the author's affections for men. He wrote to Viaud on 13 April 1904:

I feel very clearly that there is something broken between us, and it is with a sorrowful heart that I foresee the beginning of

Playbook cover for the New York City premiere of *The Daughter of Heaven*, 1912.

the end. I would, though, if I am no longer anything in your affection, like to be a little something in your friendship.[12]

The new male interest was now his aide-de-camp Osman Daney, whom he had taken with him to China.

Viaud also chose Daney to accompany him on his next military assignment, to Constantinople, at the end of 1903. When they

Osman Daney and Loti.

arrived, the author confided to his diary that the young man was 'the only being on this ship who has a place in my heart' (*Journal v*, 94). This military assignment, like the one to the Basque region over a decade before, had important consequences for Viaud's artistic output.

This time, in February 1903, the navy ordered him to command the *Vautour* (Vulture), an unglamorously named ship stationed in what was, for Viaud, a very glamorous city. His first great pleasure when he reached it on 7 September was hearing and speaking Turkish again. For Viaud, whether it was Breton, Basque, Turkish or Japanese, the local language played an important part in his interaction with the culture, even if he had only a limited command of it.

With the sound of Turkish and the familiar sights, Viaud, who is ever more subject to eruptions of past memories into consciousness, once again becomes preoccupied with his first experiences in the Ottoman Empire almost thirty years before. He thinks immediately of Hakidjé and decides that 'it is she, the beloved little dead one, who has brought me back here' (*Journal v*, 82). As he informs Juliette Adam, he decides to have her grave restored. What he does not tell Adam, however, is that he does this in part because he has had Hakidjé's headstone removed and brought back to his quarters on the *Vautour*, replacing it with a copy to disguise the theft and profanation. He will take this stela back to Rochefort and set it up in the mosque, where it remains to this day.

Viaud does also occasionally think of Mehmet during his eighteen months on the *Vautour*, and goes looking for his grave as well. He finds that the headstone, which he had had erected during his first return to the city, has been stolen. As had often been the case with the 'brothers' in his life, Viaud consoles himself with the thought that, like Hakidjé, 'this little one . . . loved me so much' (*Journal v*, 206; also 89). It is difficult to understand how someone who had been so doted upon as a child could have needed such reassurance that others loved him.

More surprisingly, given his absence from Viaud's records of his previous returns to and thoughts about Constantinople, during this lengthy Turkish sojourn the author makes an attempt to discover what had become of Daniel. In his diary pages from his first stay in the region in 1876, and even in the novel that he derived from them after censorship from Jousselin, Viaud had once told himself and even his readers that the handsome young boatman loved him a great deal as well. In February 1904, when the *Vautour* docks in what is today Thessaloníki, the city where the 26-year-old Viaud had first met him and Hakidjé, Viaud manages to track Daniel down. He finds the man he had once loved in all the muscled beauty of his youth reduced by sickness to frailty and premature old age. This makes Viaud feel 'irremediably' old himself (*Journal v*, 112). When he goes to visit him on shore, the Frenchman encounters

The stela from Hakidjé's grave, in Viaud's Rochefort mosque.

Daniel's 28-year-old 'robust' son, whom he recalls seeing as a sickly baby in the arms of his mother – a wife and child of whom there had been no mention in *Aziyadé* or even Viaud's (reworked) diary from his first sojourn in the area. At the end of the visit, for which Viaud records no emotions or recollections of what he had been to Daniel, or Daniel to him, 28 years before, the Frenchman returns to his ship and, as soon as the weather allows, orders anchor to be weighed so that he can sail back to Constantinople.

Why did he weep over Hakidjé and Mehmet but not Daniel? It must have something to do with Viaud's effort to erase his first Turkish love – however that love may have manifested itself in 1876 – from his own memory, not to mention others'. In November of the previous year he had taken a M. de Fénelon, an attaché at the French embassy in Constantinople, to see the first home he had occupied in Constantinople in 1876. He recorded in his diary, presumably repeating what he told Fénelon, that it was there, in Hasköy, 'that I had first welcomed my dear little [female] friend [Hakidjé] on her return from Salonique [Thessaloníki]; it is there that my poor Mehmed had worked so hard to arrange that room on the second floor that I still see' (*Journal v*, 90).

This is either a remarkable case of memory failure, or else a simple lie. By the time Hakidjé (and her literary manifestation, Aziyadé) arrived in Constantinople, in January 1877, Viaud/Harry Grant had already moved to his second onshore lodging, in Eyoub, a suburb of Constantinople further up the Golden Horn. More importantly, Daniel (and, in the novel, his counterpart Samuel) is the person who spent eight days cleaning the house in preparation for the young woman's arrival. Did Viaud honestly remember this episode the way he recounted it to his diary and evidently to Fénelon? Did Fénelon or his memory point out the mistake? Why, after making no mention of Daniel during his three previous returns to the area, at least in his diary and his public writings, did Viaud subsequently decide to search him out? Was it out of a sense of guilt? These are all intriguing questions for which we have no answers.

It is worth keeping in mind how much Viaud was reliving – and rewriting – his first, by now legendary, sojourn in Constantinople when considering the new adventure he had there. In April 1904, Viaud received a letter, in French, claiming to be from a young Turkish wife who was unhappy living as a virtual prisoner in her husband's harem. She wanted Viaud, who had once known such a harem dweller, Hakidjé, and her unhappiness with such a life, to speak to the world about the plight of Turkish women condemned to similar situations. Signing her letter Nour-el-Nissa, she asked Viaud to meet her in a solitary place outside the city.

He does. What he finds when he gets there is not one woman, however, but three. He meets them several more times while in Constantinople, all the while exchanging letters with the apparent spokesperson of the group, Leyla. In March 1905, he finishes his tour of duty and returns to Rochefort, where he continues the epistolary exchange. Leyla continues to recount the life of a modern harem dweller, very different from that of Hakidjé three decades before, and asks the now world-famous author and authority on Turkey to plead their case to his world. In July Viaud begins to transform their correspondence into an epistolary novel, published in England as *The Disenchanted*.[13] Then, in early January 1906, while he is still working on the book, Viaud receives a letter from one of the two other women informing him that Leyla is dead, having committed suicide in despair. Viaud is deeply moved but, having all the material he needs, keeps working.

His novelization of their correspondence begins with a preface that states:

> This is an imagined story. You would waste your time try-
> ing to give Djénane [Leyla], Zeyneb, Mélek or André [the
> Loti character in the novel] real names, because they never

existed. All that is true is the great intellectual culture spread through Turkish harems, and the suffering that results from it . . . The marvellous prophet of Islam, who was above all else a creature of light and charity, cannot want laws that he decreed in the past to become, with the inevitable evolution of time, motives for suffering. (*Disenchanted*, Preface)

In the 1 June issue of *La Revue des Deux Mondes* in which the work was being serialized, literary critic Victor Giraud hailed the novel as 'a plea for Muslim feminism'.[14] By 11 June, four days before the appearance of the last instalment, Viaud informed his diary that the work was a 'complete success' (*Journal v*, 274). In 1914 he is asked to give two lectures on 'the Turkish woman' by the founder of a new feminist publication, *La Vie feminine* (*Soldats*, p. 28).[15] By the time Viaud dies, the book has gone through 416 editions, the most of any of his works other than *Iceland Fisherman* and well ahead of the volume in third place, *Madame Chrysanthemum*, with 'only' 211. By comparison, his other novel about a Turkish harem dweller, *Aziyadé*, had gone through 201 editions by then. For someone who had appeared to have abandoned the novel after *Ramuntcho*, Viaud enjoyed a major financial and critical triumph.

It was not unalloyed. By the time he wrote that 11 June diary entry, Viaud, then in Paris, found himself with two unexpected visitors, Nouriyé and Zennour, the other two women he had met with Leyla in Constantinople. They announced that they had fled their harems at Leyla's death and now wanted Viaud's help getting established in fashionable Paris. They wrote letters to the Paris newspapers, which were delighted to discover that *The Disenchanted*'s supposedly fictional story was at least based on true current events.[16] Meanwhile, rumours from Constantinople suggested that Viaud had been the victim of at least a partial hoax, that Leyla, whoever she might have been, was not dead. Calmann-Lévy was sending Viaud sizeable royalty checks for

The Disenchanted, but the work caused him a certain amount of embarrassment.

We need to get ahead of our chronology here for a moment to follow this story to its conclusion. Viaud returned to Constantinople again in 1910. This time he had his son Samuel join him. Though they both spent most of their time in the hospital or their sickbeds, Viaud did have a chance to do some investigation regarding Leyla. Whatever he actually found, in the pages of his diary as he published them a few years later he expressed doubts but finally concluded that 'more than ever I have the impression that I will never know anything.'[17]

Those doubts were put to rest in 1924, a year after Viaud's death, when 'Leyla', in reality the French journalist Marc Hélys, published *Le Secret des 'Désenchantées'* (The Secret of the 'Disenchanted'), in which she revealed that, after having done work on her own to publicize the suffering of Turkish women confined to harems, she had gone to Constantinople, made friends with two educated young Turkish women there and, presenting themselves to Viaud as three 'awakened' young harem dwellers, had misled the well-meaning but evidently not too perceptive older author – Viaud was in his early fifties at the time – into writing a plea for Turkish women to the large audience only someone as well known as he could attract.[18] Like an ingénue in a Molière comedy, they, and especially Hélys, had pulled the wool over an infatuated older man's eyes, though in this case for a good cause. Hélys' book sold well and Viaud, no longer alive to present his side of the story, looked foolish, even though Hélys did stress in her preface that 'the beauty of *The Disenchanted* owes nothing to me. It is the genius of Loti,' which a comparison of the original letters and Viaud's transformation of them substantiates.[19]

Did Viaud really believe the story Hélys fed him in their meetings and her letters, all of which she included in her exposé? Perhaps at first, though he, who paid so much attention to language, must have been surprised that a Turkish woman who had never been to France could speak and write the language so well. Rather, I suspect that Viaud saw in this subterfuge a chance to write a novel that followed in the tracks of his previous two important fictional works, *Judith Renaudin* and *Ramuntcho*. In his reworking of the correspondence it becomes another story of society trying to control minds and a young person, or here three persons, struggling to throw off the mental yoke that was being imposed upon them. A comparison of the original correspondence with its transformation in the novel shows how hard Viaud worked to turn everyday prose into what is, in fact, an often very powerful work of art. Since it is, in part, a novel about the effect of other novels on its main female characters, it is also in the lineage of *Madame Bovary*, the masterpiece by Viaud's favourite writer, Flaubert. It is a paean to the power of literature to free the mind, and in that sense a development of the Bible-reading scene at the end of *Judith Renaudin* and Ramuntcho's reactions to the books he reads.

Nor did Viaud present just the case of Turkish women in *The Disenchanted*. As he had done with *Judith Renaudin*, he also used the story to defend the cause of gay men who had been 'enchanted' – we would say brainwashed – into believing that they needed to marry, the situation that finally drives Leyla's equivalent in the novel, Djéname, to commit suicide as it had driven Judith Renaudin to exile.[20]

After escorting Nouriyé and Zennour around Paris that day in June 1906, Viaud paid Robert de Montesquiou a visit, just as he had invited him to the dress rehearsal of *Judith Renaudin*. As too often, however Viaud's diary, at least as we have it now, does not say what Viaud wanted to tell him.

10

Loti the Turkophile (1907–14)

With the royalties from *The Disenchanted* streaming in, Viaud decided to set off on another voyage, this time to Egypt. Just as France's first illustrated magazines had filled him as a young boy with a desire to see the temples in Angkor, so they had set him to dreaming about visiting the great monuments of the kingdom of the pharaohs.

Another part of the inspiration for this trip came from Juliette Adam, who had travelled to Egypt herself several years before and met a young Egyptian who had become a leader in the nationalist movement: Mustafa Kamil (1874–1908). Through his newspaper, *The Standard*, Kamil called for the withdrawal of English troops that had been stationed in his homeland since the 1882 Anglo-Egyptian War. He also asked the khedive, Abbas Hilmi II, who governed Egypt for the Ottoman sultan more or less as a viceroy, to grant a constitution. Adam had taken Kamil to Rochefort to meet Viaud in 1902, and the two had remained in contact since.

Kamil had reason to encourage Viaud to visit his homeland. The author had spoken out in several of his works, starting with *Aziyadé*, against the European powers' attempts to seize various parts of the weakening Ottoman Empire. In his Indian travel narrative, entitled in full (in its French edition) *India (without the English)*, Viaud had repeatedly condemned the English presence in that subcontinent.

Viaud obtained six months' unpaid leave from the navy and set out from Marseille with Kamil and Osman Daney in January

A *dahabieh*, the type of boat Viaud voyaged in up the Nile.

1907. When they arrived in Cairo he found himself welcomed
by nationalists as a hero. The khedive himself received him,
though he had read *The Disenchanted*. Since Abbas Hilmi secretly
supported Kamil and the nationalists against the British, his
generous treatment of the Anglophobe French author was,
perhaps, not surprising. After the requisite visit to the Great
Pyramids and the Sphynx, Viaud and his companions caught
a train that took them up the Nile to a *dahabieh*, a sort of yacht
specifically designed for travel on the river which the khedive
had had outfitted for him in luxurious manner. Viaud spent
a month sailing up the Nile to Philae, two islands famous for
their beautifully preserved temples dating from the pharaohs
through to the Roman occupation. Another of Viaud's reasons
for undertaking the trip – and another of Kamil's reasons for
supporting it – was that this important historical site was now
subject to flooding because of the Aswan Low Dam, which the
British had constructed in 1902. (The temples would continue
to be flooded until the 1960s, when UNESCO undertook a vast
project to save some of them.) After a visit to the temples under

moonlight on 3 March, Viaud and Daney sailed back to Cairo, Alexandria and then France.

There Viaud took time to transform the sparse text in his diary into often beautifully crafted pages evoking the poetic splendour of the Nile Valley. Calmann-Lévy released the book form, *La Mort de Philae* (The Death of Philae; in W. P. Baines's English translation simply *Egypt*), in January 1909. It became the bestselling of all Viaud's travel narratives, reaching 105 editions by his death in 1923. Readers saw that it was as much, if not more, an exercise in painting than a photographic reproduction of reality. Jean Schlumberger, for example, lauded its 'delicate harmonizations', the same term art critics were using to describe Monet's latest, more complex canvases.[1]

The work's title, *The Death of Philae*, suggests that someone was killing beauty in Egypt. Viaud's originally proposed name for the work, *Egypt Invaded* in English, had been even more blunt. It recalls the remarks about the Industrial Powers' invasion of China after the Boxer Rebellion that he had omitted when he turned his diary into *The Last Days of Peking*. Claude Martin, the editor of a volume of Viaud's travel narratives, has suggested that the author reconsidered his wording this time because he had been invited to visit London in July 1909 and be received by Edward VII and Queen Alexandra.[2]

The six-month leave of absence to visit Egypt did nothing to improve Viaud's standing with the navy hierarchy. He was informed that upon his sixtieth birthday, 14 January 1910, he would be irrevocably retired. Thereafter, all his world travel would be as a private citizen.

The first of these voyages took place later that same year. Still troubled by rumours that 'Leyla''s story had been a hoax, Viaud made his sixth trip to Constantinople in large part in order to learn the truth. Back in Rochefort he showed no rush to transform his diary pages into another travel narrative. He did not start until

1913 or 1914 and did not send them off to a magazine, this time *L'Illustration*, until the next year.

This may have been in part because what really held his attention after his return from Constantinople in late 1910 was politics, specifically the various European powers' designs on the Ottoman Empire. When Italy declared war on it in September 1911, hoping to capture Tripolitania (modern Libya), Viaud started publishing articles in *Le Figaro* and elsewhere condemning the attack and defending the Turks. By early 1913 there were enough such articles to comprise a small volume, *Turquie agonisante* (Turkey on its Deathbed). While he had been a naval officer, Viaud had been required, at least nominally, to submit his publications to the Navy for approval, though that didn't always happen. Now he was free to publish as he chose, and he chose to become the western European defender of the Turks.

Once he started, he didn't want to stop. *Turkey on Its Deathbed* sold well enough to justify subsequent editions that year. Viaud kept writing more chapters, including a defence of Turkish massacres of Armenians. These were not the wholesale slaughter that started in 1915, but earlier attacks. Viaud's Turkophilia came to blind him, and some of the pieces in this book are not easy to digest.

They made him even more popular with the Turks, however. He returned to Constantinople in 1913 after the publication of *Turkey on Its Deathbed*, and this time received a hero's welcome even greater than the one accorded him in Egypt six years before. Yet again he made his pilgrimage to Hakidjé's tomb, but this time there were no further efforts to learn the truth about Leyla.

When he was not travelling, Viaud found life in Rochefort lonely and unhappy. His wife Blanche, who had been isolated by deafness from the beginning of their marriage, not to mention by Viaud's lack of attention, was further closed in by weakening eyesight. When Viaud returned from a trip to Brittany in 1907 – where he had gone, among other reasons, for a romantic rendezvous with an unnamed woman – he found Blanche 'stretched out, as always, in the darkness'. 'Oh, how sad my house is,' he added, not stopping to consider how he might have contributed to that sadness (*Journal v*, 329). In his logbook entry for 2 December 1911, Viaud's personal secretary Gaston Mauberger wrote that by then

> Madame P. Loti is demented. This is the second time
> in two years, but this time the crises are terrible. When
> these crises subside, she is aggressive, nasty. She who
> was so sweet, who had a singing voice, now appears like
> a demon, a fury, with a stentorian voice. Obscene words
> even come from her mouth. But she is above all nasty.[3]

A year later Viaud described his wife to Mauberger as 'a wild crazy woman' (*une folle furieuse*).[4] She began to spend more time at her mother's home in the Dordogne region, east of Bordeaux. She died there in 1940.

Things were no better with his other 'wife'. Also in 1912 Mauberger recorded that Viaud spoke to him about 'the abominable character' of Crucita, whom, like Blanche but even more so, Viaud had caused to be cut off from her original surroundings and isolated. 'It's true', Viaud conceded to his secretary, 'she's neurasthenic at the moment,' a term used to describe what was imagined to be a collapse of the nervous system. 'And she's suffering. Maybe it's because of her age. [She was only 45 in 1911.] But she is so intolerable that I'm not going to visit her anymore. I'll have my sons come visit me.'[5]

On 30 December 1911, Viaud invited those two sons and Samuel to dinner – without their mothers – in his home in Rochefort. He recorded the dinner in his diary but did not speculate on how the three young men may have felt. It is not hard to understand why Samuel, after he inherited the house, sold off many of his father's things and demolished several of the exotic time-travel rooms.

Viaud's sister, Marie, with whom as a young man he had shared his passion for art, also became estranged from him in these years. When she passed away in 1908, Viaud's several pages of diary entries made no reference to their past conversations and exchanges.

The only relationships that remained cheerful were those with his friends in art. Though Prince Albert banished her from Monaco in 1902 because of her affair with English composer Isidore de Lara (born Isidore Cohen), Viaud still saw Princess Alice regularly when she was in France. He also saw Juliette Adam and Sarah Bernhardt on occasion, but stayed in touch with them mostly by correspondence. There were also the numerous unnamed women with whom he had trysts. 'My greatest ambition in life has been not to get old,' he confided to Mauberger in 1910.[6] These women, whatever else they may have done for him, let Viaud believe for a moment when in their arms that he had succeeded.

So did a man, but in a different, non-erotic fashion. As we have seen, ever since the humiliating defeat of the Franco-Prussian War in 1870, many Frenchmen had been convinced that their fellow countrymen had grown weak from an emphasis on culture, fine food and the other refinements of civilization. One of the individuals to profit from this conviction was Edmond Desbonnet (1868–1953), who achieved great success in the first decade of the new century with his supposedly scientific approach to bodybuilding.

'Prof. Desbonnet', as he styled himself, opened a successful gym in Paris in 1899 but made his fame with several photograph- and drawing-filled books designed to show Frenchmen how to become 'real men' and prepare themselves for their patriotic duty in the next war. Viaud, who had devoted himself to bodybuilding since his twenties, became a fan and friend. He began to see Desbonnet regularly around 1909, when he wrote a preface to the Professor's latest profusely illustrated instructional manual, *How One Becomes an Athlete*. In a book full of 250 drawings and photographs of fig-leaf-wearing men shown 'before and after' they followed the Professor's

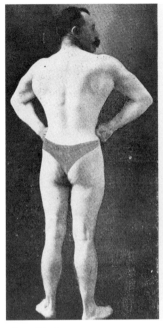

Edmond Desbonnet.

regimen, there is something comical about the title page, which announces the presence of a preface by 'Pierre Loti of the French Academy', followed two pages later by a full-page photo of the author in his academic regalia. Desbonnet listed all his own credentials at the top of the title page, including 'Doctor of Medicine' and 'Doctor of Science' from New York, but lest that not suffice to convince 45-kilo weaklings and 135-kilo monuments to self-indulgence to buy his book, Academician Viaud provided extra support. As superficial as it may be, Desbonnet's choice of prefacer is an indication of Viaud's standing not just as an author but as a personage in the France of this decade.

Between the women and the exercise, Viaud felt vigorous. In July 1912, he staged another operatic performance in his home,

Un type d'athlète complet : Le Pugilateur DAMOXENE, de Canova

Title page from Edmond Desbonnet's *Comment on devient Athlète*.

again featuring excerpts from Meyerbeer's *The Huguenots*, about the Catholic massacre of Protestants in sixteenth-century France. It was part of a musical evening in honour of his guest, Princess Alice, who was there with her English lover, de Lara. Mauberger sent an account of it to the Paris newspapers. At one point the director of the Théâtre Rochefort emerged to announce that the tenor for the Act v trio from *The Huguenots* was indisposed. Fortunately, he continued, the master of the house had consented to assume the role of Raoul de Nangis, the Protestant leader who, at the end of the opera, is killed as part of the St Bartholomew's Day Massacre. Mauberger's article goes on to praise the ease with which Viaud acquitted himself of the music, and to note that 'his disconcerting youth under Raoul's violet velvet doublet was enchanting.'[7]

The story of the indisposed tenor was a lie, of course. Viaud had been rehearsing the trio for days. The evening of the performance, he circulated among his guests in Raoul de Nangis' costume. In part, no doubt, he wanted to show off in Raoul's traditional form-filling doublet his torso as it had been sculpted by Prof. Desbonnet's exercises. In part, however, fourteen years after *Judith Renaudin*, Viaud was still associating himself with those of his ancestors and their fellow Protestants who had been persecuted by an intolerant society for being different and refusing to conform.

11
Diplomat and War Correspondent (1914–18)

On 28 June 1914, Serbian nationalist Gavrilo Princip assassinated Austrian Archduke Franz Ferdinand, setting off the First World War. France began mobilizing the following month.

Viaud tried to reactivate his service. As he told Gaston Mauberger: 'I'll settle for being a lieutenant again, if they want. [He had held the rank of captain when he was forced into retirement.] If I were just Capt. Julien Viaud, I wouldn't say anything. But I'm Loti, and I have to set an example.'[1] The navy agreed to enlist him in August, but sent him back home the next month. Not willing to give up, Viaud did the unthinkable and appealed to the army. They appointed him liaison agent – without pay – to General Joseph Gallieni. A year older than Viaud, Gallieni had just been called back to active duty to serve as military governor of Paris. It was under his orders that Paris taxi cabs 'saved France', transporting extra troops to the First Battle of the Marne.

Viaud's initial assignment was to convince the Ottoman Empire not to enter the war on the side of the Triple Alliance: Germany, Austria-Hungary and Italy. The Turks had good reason to hate the English, French and Russians, the Triple Entente, all of whom had been making inroads into the Ottoman Empire since Viaud was sent with the French navy to Salonica and Constantinople in 1876. They had similar cause to hate the Austrians and Italians, however. Despite Viaud's efforts, the Turks allied with Germany and attacked Russia in October. Viaud's reaction was egotistic:

'It's the end of Constantinople, which will be annihilated in oceans of blood. It's the end of my memories and my youth' (*Soldats*, p. 51). Gallieni entrusted him with convincing the sultan, Mehmed v, not to expand the Ottoman Empire's attacks to the rest of the Entente, but it was too late. Because of their system of secret alliances, once the Turks attacked Russia, Great Britain and France declared war on the Turks, who promptly declared war on them.

Viaud's other wartime assignment was to use the press to depict the horrors of the German invasion of northern France in a way that would turn the world against the invader. Since he was stationed in Paris, it was easy for him to make trips to the front lines, from where he wrote vehemently anti-German articles, in particular for *L'Illustration*. That allowed him to accompany his fiery prose with sometimes horrifying or heart-wrenching photographs.

One of the best examples of this is his 21 November 1914 *L'Illustration* article 'The Phantom Cathedral', a eulogy for the great cathedral in Reims that had recently been bombed. Almost a century before, in his novel *Notre-Dame de Paris* (in English, usually *The Hunchback of Notre-Dame*), Victor Hugo had used an old, largely abandoned medieval cathedral as a symbol of France's glorious and noble past, an era when artistic giants built monumental works for the ages – not unlike what Viaud had done several years before for Egypt in *The Death of Philae*. (In fact, Viaud even compared the charred ruins of Reims Cathedral to 'a large mummy, still standing straight and majestic'.[2]) Then, in the 1890s, Monet had followed suit with his series of thirty-some paintings depicting the great cathedral in Rouen. For these artists, the nation's Gothic cathedrals were not relics of a dying faith. They were manifestations of the French people, who, Hugo had claimed, still felt attached to these masterpieces built by their own ancestors.

Viaud took the same tack in describing the ruins of Reims Cathedral. In keeping with the Impressionists, who had rejected the École des Beaux-Arts emphasis on copying Italian Renaissance

Claude Monet, *Rouen Cathedral: The Portal (Sunlight)*, 1894, oil on canvas.

Loti in infantry uniform during the First World War.

masters like Raphael, he asserted that the cathedral was 'lighter and more soaring' because it was constructed before the arrival in France of 'the sensual heaviness of what people now call the Renaissance', a style that came from Italy 'to make everything materialistic and spoil it'.[3] If the Germans, the 'barbarians', had spent years preparing to bomb this masterpiece, it was because they understood that the cathedral was 'the very heart of old France'.[4]

And what was the 'very heart of France'? For Viaud, the creator of fantasy time-travel machines in his home in Rochefort, Reims Cathedral and other masterpieces like it taught the French how to soar in their minds above the material modern world like the 'mysterious artists of the thirteenth century' who had built these monuments 'in meditation and dream'.[5] Such initiators of dreams could not be constructed today, Viaud suggested, but they remained at the heart of what was still best in the French 'race'.[6]

This was what the government wanted. On 7 September 1915, Viaud was invited to tour the wreckage of Soissons Cathedral. The following month he published an article about it. On 25 October he was asked to read it before the French Academy and an audience of notables. He did so not in his Academic regalia but in his military officer's uniform, to great applause. Like the best correspondents covering any war, Viaud recounted not simply the facts, but who the French were and why that was worth fighting for.[7] As the war proceeded, Viaud gathered the magazine pieces in which he did this into volumes, of which Calmann-Lévy published three. They were the only books Viaud published during the war. Only the first, *La Hyène enragée* (The Mad Hyena), has been translated into English, using the less colourful title *War*.

If Viaud could not get enough of the war himself, wanting to remain as close to the fighting as possible, he was saddened to see his three sons enlist, especially Samuel. After years of comparing him unfavourably to the two Basque boys as feeble and lazy, the author now found respect for his oldest son, and even love. When he saw him at Christmas in Rochefort he wondered if the young man would return from the war and described him as 'my whole reason for living' (*Soldats*, p. 54). Even Osman Daney, whom Viaud managed to obtain as his aide-de-camp, ranked after Samuel in his affections: 'his absence also breaks my heart' (*Soldats*, p. 54). By 1917 Edmond and Raymond seemed distant from him. 'No,' he told his diary in April, 'my son Samuel is the only one who counts for me, and he is at the front!' (*Soldats*, pp. 149–50).

In 1916 Viaud requested to be sent to Verdun, site of one of the largest and longest battles of the war. Gallieni had recently died, so he was assigned to General Philippe Pétain, who would later be hailed as 'the hero of Verdun'. Viaud felt 'antipathy' for him the first time they met (*Soldats*, p. 117). The feeling was evidently mutual. Hindsight would read this in Viaud's favour, since Pétain became France's number one collaborator with the Nazis in the Second World War. Viaud was still able to carry out several reconnaissance missions, and did his best to bring Spain and Romania into the war on the side of the Entente, since he knew the queens of both. Romania was willing, since it wanted to seize territory from the Austro-Hungarian Empire. Spain remained neutral.

In 1917 Viaud managed to be reassigned to General Louis Franchet d'Espèrey, who was then in charge of the Northern Army Group. Franchet d'Espèrey had served in several of the same campaigns as Viaud, including Indochina and China. Like Viaud, he was also rumoured to be homosexual. The author reported getting along well with him, and even dedicated one of his collections of newspaper articles about the war, *L'Horreur allemande* (The German Horror, 1918), to him, but his reason for requesting the post was that it allowed him to remain close to Samuel, who was serving in the same area. The next May, Franchet d'Espèrey ordered Viaud to stand down from the front, warning him that he was pushing himself beyond his strength. In June Viaud was awarded the Croix de Guerre. The citation read:

Although he was exempt because of his age from any
military service, [Viaud] resumed service from the
beginning of the war, thereby giving the finest example
of devotion and patriotism. [He] completed under
enemy fire . . . several missions, which he acquitted to the
complete satisfaction of his chiefs (*Soldats*, pp. 270–1).

The 68-year-old Viaud had a right to be happy, but he was not.
Back home in Rochefort, when he learned of this honour he told
his diary: 'I hardly dare believe it, I am so unaccustomed to having
even slight joy' (*Soldats*, p. 248). Instead, he just felt lonely.

12

Last Years (1919–23)

One of the collateral advantages of the First World War for the
victors was that it gave them an excuse to carve up the Ottoman
Empire and divide the spoils among themselves and their Arab
allies, something they had started to do before 1914. In the Treaty
of Sèvres they proposed reducing the Ottoman Empire to little
more than the territory around Constantinople. The Young Turks,
the Turkish Nationalist Movement, rebelled against this and
forced a new arrangement, laid out in the Treaty of Lausanne. It
established the Republic of Turkey as we know it today, but still
divided up the rest of the former empire.

For Viaud this was unacceptable. In a stream of articles
that appeared in 1919–20 in France's leading newspapers and
magazines, he argued that France needed the Ottomans as future
allies and should respect their empire. The powers who drew up the
treaties did not listen. In fact, his journalism so angered the British
that they changed a street named after him to Georges Clemenceau
Road. In what was becoming Turkey, however, he was hailed as a
national hero. In 1921 the nationalist founder of the new republic,
Mustafa Kemal Atatürk, sent a delegation to Rochefort. It informed
Viaud that 'the smallest [Turkish] children know your name and
pronounce it like the name of God.'[1]

In these years Viaud also penned a sequel of sorts to *The Story
of a Child* entitled *First Youth*, which came out in 1919. As we saw in
the first chapters of this volume, some of it appears to have been an

attempt to rewrite Viaud's adolescence in the form in which he now wanted it to be remembered: heterosexual but chaste. In this sense, it was his equivalent of the Egyptian monuments he had described so romantically in *The Death of Philae*. Also like the pharaohs, Viaud became preoccupied with his own death and repeatedly gave instructions to Mauberger and others regarding what should be placed with him in his coffin.

Like the pharaohs as well, Viaud had to contend with those who wanted to profane his monuments and the memory they were designed to perpetuate. He reported to Mauberger that his sister Marie's daughter, Ninette Duvignau, was writing a book that would 'demolish' *First Youth* and recount 'all sorts of gossip' about him.[2]

His son Samuel married a vice-admiral's daughter in 1920. Thereafter, he grew more distant from his father. By October of that year Alice Barthou, the wife of a former prime minister and one of Viaud's last devoted friends, informed Mauberger that Samuel and his new wife 'were of no help to their father'.[3] Viaud was proud of Raymond once again; he had entered the merchant marine and seemed to be doing well. It is interesting that when Viaud interceded to get him hired on a ship in the Messageries Maritimes line, their reply referred to the young man as 'Raymond Viaud'.[4] Viaud had never legally recognized either of his Basque sons and never would. Is that how Raymond Gainza now presented himself?

On 10 April 1921, Viaud suffered an attack that left him paralysed on his left side. He could no longer write, and for a while his speech was impaired. He nonetheless kept working on revisions to pages in his diary from the 1913 trip to Constantinople that he wanted to include in *Suprêmes Visions d'Orient* (Supreme Visions of the East), which was to cover his last two sojourns there. Now he had to dictate the revisions to Mauberger, however. The book was published in September and sold remarkably well. By then it described a Constantinople that was at least eight years old and already fading into legend.

Sarah Bernhardt died in March 1923. When Viaud learned this, his already poor health declined further. 'Before dying myself,' he told Mauberger, 'I will have experienced all the sorrows life has to offer.'[5] At the end of April, fearing that his own end was close, he asked Juliette Adam, then 87, to pay him a visit. She did, and managed to calm him. A few days later he requested to be taken to the grotto near La Roche Courbon where, according to *First Youth*, the young gypsy had first introduced him to sex. 'He lost himself in a long reverie,' Mauberger recorded.[6] Since it would appear that the gypsy story was a fabrication, we can only wonder what Viaud remembered, or thought he remembered, having taken place there fifty-some years before. Was he convincing himself of the legends he was forging about himself?

Viaud asked to make one more trip to his house in Hendaye. There, on 10 June, while the sunlight streamed over him as it had over Sylvestre in *Iceland Fisherman*, Julien Viaud died. He was accorded a state funeral, at which Léo Thémèze and Osman Daney were among the pallbearers. Viaud's coffin was carried by a naval vessel to Oléron island, off the shore from Rochefort, where his mother's family had lived before moving to the city.[7] Viaud wanted to be buried in a place that he had associated in *Judith Renaudin* with a minority that was persecuted for being different and an individual who was pressured to marry. In accord with his wishes, Samuel returned the next day and dug up the coffin so as to break holes in it that would permit earth to enter as the body decomposed. Eventually his father would be one with nature. Some of what Viaud had learned in India two decades before had remained with him.

13

Life after Death (1923–?)

No author was more concerned about cheating death than Julien Viaud. He seemed to find a kinship with the pharaohs whose tombs he visited in Egypt; he, too, devoted much effort not only to publicizing his image, but to shaping it for posterity. As with the children he fathered with Crucita Gainza, it was Pierre Loti the person whose survival seemed to concern him most. Both the legitimate and the illegitimate lines have now died out, however. The effort to survive physically in this world was futile.

For a time after his death it looked as if his literary survival might suffer the same fate. In part there were political issues. Viaud's unwavering support of the Turks during the Armenian massacres that started in 1915 did not sit well with liberal Westerners. Meanwhile, French literature kept innovating. Though in the best of his novels Viaud had demonstrated some of the techniques that were subsequently practised by the writers who became important in the 1920s, like Marcel Proust, these were not the things that had made him famous, so readers of serious literature looked elsewhere for them.

Several things happened in the 1970s and '80s to revive interest in his work, for better but also worse. Roland Barthes' preface to *Aziyadé* attracted attention among a crowd that was eager to discover the latest innovation in literature. Though some of the essay is superficial and demonstrates an ignorance of the actual publication of the novel – it appeared anonymously, not under the name Pierre Loti, as Barthes claimed – it does nevertheless highlight Viaud's early efforts to break down the monolithic narrative voice in traditional nineteenth-century French fiction. Though Barthes' essay is often cited, literary studies did not pursue its examination of Viaud's narrative innovations.

Instead, it was the literary critical milestone that appeared at the end of the 1970s, Edward Said's *Orientalism*, that brought Viaud's work back to the attention of literary scholars in the United States and England. It gave rise to dissertations by literature scholars-in-training that applied what Said had done to whatever texts these students could find that dealt with the non-Western world, including several of Viaud's early novels.

This coincided with a change in scholarly publishing. As university presses, the primary outlet for literature dissertations turned into first books, were now expected to lose less money, they made it known that they saw more likelihood of selling a literature monograph if it dealt with several authors rather than just one. Parallel with this, there was a shift in graduate literary training in the United States that focused more on theory and its application to literature rather than the traditional approach of specializing in one author, no matter how minor.

As a result, starting in the 1980s, six-chapter books began appearing from scholarly presses in the United States in which, in one of those chapters, one or two of Viaud's less important novels – *Aziyadé*, *The Marriage of Loti*, *The Story of a Spahi*, or *Madame Chrysanthemum* – were used to denounce the not surprising fact that Viaud shared some of the racial prejudices of his time. Too often, those dissertators did not delve deeper to see in what ways those early Viaud texts did not adhere to the racism of their era.

The market for such studies is largely limited to other academics, so the damage the more extreme ones might have inflicted on Viaud's standing with the general reading public has been limited. The most unfortunate result is that they have convinced some who teach French literature to college students that Viaud was a just another bigoted colonialist author and can be dismissed as such. Nor do they consider the more general question of whether we are to jettison all literature that does not share our own twenty-first-century enlightened views, even when that literature was written during eras when virtually no one benefited from such enlightenment.

French academic literary criticism has been less caught up in passing moral judgements. That may explain why Gallimard and Flammarion, two of France's most prestigious publishers, began in those same 1980s to bring out annotated editions of Viaud's novels, often edited by Bruno Vercier, one of today's two great Loti scholars. This has made Viaud's best works available to a general francophone audience in editions that situate his work in its historical and literary contexts. The 1980s also marked the first appearance of Alain Quella-Villéger's thoroughly documented and researched biography, *Pierre Loti l'incompris* (Paris, 1986), since revised as *Le Pèlerin de la planète* (Bordeaux, 1998). It has given at least francophone readers a chance to discover the differences between Viaud and the personas he created for public consumption. Our knowledge of Viaud's life has been augmented since 2006 with the appearance of Quella-Villéger and Vercier's monumental edition of Viaud's diary.

Like the work of every other pre-twenty-first-century author I know, Viaud's is not free of prejudice, though it is often more open-minded than that of most of his male contemporaries. Viaud was interested in getting to know the inhabitants and cultures of several of the lands in which he lived, not just laughing at their differences, and this contributed to his open-mindedness. The best of his work demonstrates that interest. It also considers the role of memory and art in life and literature, and the importance of freedom of thought – issues that concern us more as we get older. If these issues concern you, you will enjoy picking up some of his best work now that you are ready to put this volume down.

References

Introduction

1 Henry James, 'Pierre Loti', in *Literary Criticism: French Writers, Other European Writers, the Prefaces to the New York Edition*, ed. Leon Edel (New York, 1984), pp. 482, 505, 516. For a study of James's views on Viaud's works see Barbara Melchiori, 'Feelings about Aspects: Henry James on Pierre Loti', *Studi americani*, XV (1969), pp. 169–99.

2 James Woodress, *Willa Cather: A Literary Life* (Lincoln, NE, 1987), p. 189; L. Brent Bohlke and Sharon Hoover, eds, *Willa Cather Remembered* (Lincoln, NE, 2002), p. 45.

3 Pierre Loti, *Discours de réception à l'Académie française* (Paris, 1892), p. 61. This oration was printed the day after he delivered it in newspapers throughout France, sometimes on the front page, thereby reaching pretty much any current or potential French reader of Viaud's works.

4 André Suarès, 'Loti', in *Présences* (Paris, 1926), p. 212.

5 Franck Ferrand, 'Rochefort: Pierre Loti's Planet', *France Today* (March 2007), p. 17.

6 Eve Kosofsky Sedgwick, *Epistemology of the Closet* (Berkeley, CA, 1990), p. 165.

7 On Wilde's creation of a public persona, see for example Shelton Waldrep, *The Aesthetics of Self-invention: Oscar Wilde to David Bowie* (Minneapolis, MN, 2004).

1 The Idyllic Years (1850–65)

1 Alain Quella-Villéger, *Pierre Loti: Le Pèlerin de la planète* (Bordeaux, 1998), p. 28. This is by far the best biography of Viaud. It is not, however, available in English.

2 On Marie Viaud's work as an artist see Odette Valence and Samuel
   Pierre-Loti-Viaud, *La Famille de Pierre Loti; ou L'Éducation passionnée*
   (Paris, 1940), Part II, Ch. 2. On the transformation of a room in
   the Viaud family home to create a studio for her see Alain Quella-
   Villéger, *Chez Pierre Loti: Une maison d'écrivain-voyageur* (n.p., 2008),
   p. 13.

3 Valence and Pierre-Loti-Viaud, *La Famille de Pierre Loti*, p. 60.

4 Daniel Wildenstein, Monet correspondence, letter 719. Monet's
   correspondence was published by Wildenstein at the end of the
   various volumes of his first catalogue raisonné of the painter's work,
   Claude Monet: Biographie et catalogue raisonné, 5 vols (Lausanne,
   1974–91). I refer to this edition in my citations as 'Wildenstein,
   Monet correspondence' and reference the painter's letters by the
   numbers assigned them in the catalogue, since the pages are very
   large, the print small, and there are often many letters on a page.
   The verb that I have translated here as 'to enjoy', *jouir*, has erotic
   connotations in French: it can mean to have an orgasm. Such
   eroticism was not foreign to Monet's understanding of how he and,
   perhaps, the viewers of his paintings could react to the beauty he saw
   in nature, as the vocabulary he used to describe what he experienced
   when painting – ardour, desire, obsession, passion – demonstrates.

2 Times of Crisis, Times of Decision (1865–6)

1 As Irene L. Szyliowicz wrote in the book she derived from her
   dissertation, the gypsy girl 'appears as little more than a pastiche of
   commonplaces', *Pierre Loti and the Oriental Woman* (New York, 1962),
   p. 62.

2 When *First Youth* was published in 1919 the episode with the gypsy
   'shocked some prudish people', Viaud's personal secretary Gaston
   Mauberger noted. Whether this wording was Mauberger's or Viaud's
   is not clear. Gaston Mauberger, *Dans l'intimité de Pierre Loti (1903–
   1923)*, ed. Alain Quella-Villéger (Saintes, 2003), p. 319. Szyliowicz
   wrote of the description of the grotto entrance in front of which the
   two have sex: 'more explicit "vagina dentata" imagery could hardly
   be forthcoming' (*Oriental Woman*, p. 61). This is part of her attempt

to portray Viaud as a misogynist, for which I don't find any support in his diary or his works.

3 Paris in the 1860s

1 On the French rediscovery of Rembrandt see Alison McQueen, *The Rise of the Cult of Rembrandt: Reinventing an Old Master in Nineteenth-century France* (Amsterdam, 2003). The topic is also discussed in Chapter Eight of this volume with reference to Viaud's novel *Ramuntcho*. On the French art establishment's fixation on the Italian masters, see for example Ross King, *The Judgment of Paris* (New York, 2006).
2 Anka Muhlstein, 'Painters and Writers: When Something New Happens', *New York Review of Books*, LXIV/1 (2017), p. 33.

4 In the Navy (1867–77)

1 These three volumes were published by Calmann-Lévy as *A Poor Young Officer* (1923), covering 1867–78, and two volumes of *Private Diary*: *vol. I: 1878–81* (pub. 1925) and *vol. II: 1882–5* (pub. 1929). The first of the three appeared in English as *Notes of My Youth*.
2 Robert A. Nye, *Masculinity and Male Codes of Honor in Modern France* (Berkeley, CA, 1993), p. 74.
3 Ibid. p. 77.
4 On this see Krzysztof Pomian, 'Francs et Gaulois', in *Les Lieux de mémoire*, ed. Pierre Nora (Paris, 1992), vol. III, pp. 41–105.
5 On the rise of interest in the Celts in general and Vercingetorix in particular during the second half of the nineteenth century, see for example Paul M. Martin, *Vercingétorix: Le politique, le stratège* (Paris, 2000).
6 Odette Valence and Samuel Pierre-Loti-Viaud, *La Famille de Pierre Loti, ou L'Éducation passionnée* (Paris, 1940), p. 146.
7 Maurice E. Chernowitz, *Proust and Painting* (New York, 1945), pp. 165–6.
8 For this Viaud drawing and others like it see: *Pierre Loti dessinateur: Une oeuvre au long cours*, ed. Alain Quella-Villéger and Bruno Vercier

(Saint-Pourçain-sur-Sioule, 2009), pp. 52–3. The original, 34 by 21 cm, was held by Viaud's grandson Jacques Loti-Viaud, who was kind enough to make a full-size copy of it for me.

9 In his study of Viaud's novels, Clive Wake asserted that the author's use of the term 'brother' for Bernard and others to come 'purifies their intimacy and apparently obscures its sexual overtones', *The Novels of Pierre Loti* (The Hague, 1974), p. 32. It does not seem to have done so for Marie.

10 Quella-Villéger and Vercier present this as one of the passages that no longer exists in the Viaud diary manuscript. It appears in Pierre-Oliver Combelles' book *L'Île de Pâques: Journal d'un aspirant de La Flore* (Ville-d'Avray, 1988), pp. 44–5. Combelles wrote that he copied it directly from one of the diary notebooks (p. 21), so it was evidently still part of the whole set in 1988.

11 Since earlier in this entry Viaud wrote 'And still today, I can't think about that night without terror', it would seem that this was one passage written some time after the events described.

12 Wake, *The Novels of Pierre Loti*, p. 20.

13 On the possible Tahitian origins of the name Loti see, for example, Anne-Dominique Grenouilleau, 'Le nom de Loti et le vocabulaire tahitien dans *Le Mariage de Loti*', *Revue Pierre Loti*, 7 (July–September 1981).

14 Valence and Pierre-Loti-Viaud, *La Famille de Pierre Loti*, p. 187.

15 Viaud reused this passage, which seems to have been written later than the regular daily entries, in *Aziyadé*, Part II, Ch. 5. We will discuss that novel in the next chapter.

16 There was no standard French transcription for the young woman's name, of course. Over time, Viaud spelled it half a dozen different ways in his diary: Hakidjé, Ahkidgé, and so on.

17 Amazingly, most of this passage survived, albeit edited, in *Aziyadé*, Part I, Ch. 14.

18 Lesley Blanch, *Pierre Loti, the Legendary Romantic: A Biography* (New York, 1983), p. 109. Here, as throughout her romanticized biography, Blanch does not distinguish between the historical Viaud and the autobiographically based characters in his books.

19 Alec G. Hargreaves asserted that Viaud's 'conceptual framework, pre-occupations and value system . . . owed virtually nothing to non-European cultures', *The Colonial Experience in French Fiction* (London,

1981), p. 80, but the changes the author underwent while living in Constantinople would appear to belie that.

20 On the beginnings of positive gay writing in French literature, see Christopher Robinson, *Scandal in the Ink* (New York, 1995).

21 On this see Nye, *Masculinity*.

22 On what was being written about homosexuals in these medical journals see, for example, Vernon A. Rosario, 'Inversion's Histories / History's Inversions: Novelizing Fin-de-siècle Homosexuality', in *Science and Homosexualities*, ed. Vernon A. Rosario (New York, 1997), pp. 89–107.

23 On modern Viaud scholars' description of same-sex desire as a perversion see, for example, Keith G. Millward, *L'Oeuvre de Pierre Loti et l'esprit 'fin de siècle'* (Paris, 1955), pp. 166, 168; Irene L. Szyliowicz, *Pierre Loti and the Oriental Woman* (New York, 1988), pp. 58, 87.

24 See *Journal I*, 278. This passage does not appear in *Aziyadé*. Neither does the one several pages later when, after a rendezvous with Hakidjé on a boat in the harbour to which Daniel had rowed him, Viaud gazes at the sleeping young man and, admiring the 'antique beauty' of his head, exclaims: 'I forgot Hakidjé while thinking about the strange link that united me with this man' (*Journal I*, p. 282).

25 These lines are omitted from the corresponding episode in *Aziyadé*, Part II, Ch. 7.

26 These lines survived in *Aziyadé*, Part II, Ch. 25.

27 This part of this letter did not appear with the rest in *Aziyadé*, Part II, Ch. 24.

28 This does appear in *Aziyadé*, Part IV, Ch. 27.

5 A Successful Author – and Alter-ego – Is Born (1877–81)

1 In their book on Viaud, *La Famille de Pierre Loti; ou L'Éducation passionnée* (Paris, 1940), Viaud's legitimate son, Samuel, and a family friend, Odette Valence, claimed that Viaud's love for Hakidjé 'did not take on all its force, all its nostalgic sweetness, until the young sailor had returned to France' (p. 201).

2 Bruno Vercier and Alain Quella-Villéger, eds, *Bruno Vercier et Alain Quella-Villéger présentent 'Aziyadé' suivi de 'Fantôme d'Orient' de Pierre*

Loti (Paris, 2001), p. 172. This letter is fascinating for its dishonesty: Viaud tells Aucante that manuscript B is a work 'created and revised by M. Jousselin himself, based on notes that I wrote in haste last year in Constantinople' (p. 172), whereas, as we have seen, B was initially Viaud's extensive revision of his diary with Polignac's help.

3 There is no critical edition of *Aziyadé* showing what passage came from which manuscript at what point. The best one can do is read the relevant passages in the new edition of the diary and compare them with the novel, though that does not show who created the subsequent differences when.

4 On the number of editions of his works published during Viaud's lifetime see N. Serban, *Pierre Loti: Sa vie et son oeuvre* (Paris, 1924), pp. 338–53. For the illustrated editions of his novels see Richard M. Berrong, 'Les Editions illustrées des romans de Pierre Loti', *Le Bulletin de l'Association internationale des amis de Pierre Loti*, 15 (2006), pp. 2–13, and 'Addendum' in ibid., 16 (2007), pp. 6–8.

5 Roland Barthes, 'Pierre Loti: *Aziyadé*', in *New Critical Essays*, trans. Richard Howard (New York, 1980), pp. 105–21.

6 Marie-Paule de Saint-Léger objected that 'it is difficult for us to share [Barthes'] approach [to *Aziyadé*], which is essentially centred on homosexuality', *Pierre Loti l'insaisissable* (Paris, 1996), p. 10. That is an inaccurate description of Barthes' essay, which has its extravagances but is more complex than that. I have provided the reference to the English-language edition in the bibliography, so readers can see for themselves.

7 Edward W. Said, *Orientalism* (New York, 1978).

8 T. Denean Sharpley-Whiting, for example, declared on the basis of her reading of just one early novel, *The Story of a Spahi*, that 'if ever there was a nineteenth-century novelist . . . who wholly exemplified the colonialist mentality of his era, it was Pierre Loti', *Sexualized Savages, Primal Fears, and Primitive Narratives in French* (Durham, NC, 1999), p. 91.

9 See Chapter Nine of this book, n. 13, about the meaning of this title.

10 Irene L. Szyliowicz, convinced that 'homosexuals . . . frequently need to vilify women as a compensatory mechanism to deal with their guilt for their own sexual persuasions', declared that 'clearly Loti needs to debase women in order to assert his masculine superiority,' *Pierre Loti*

and the Oriental Woman (New York, 1988), pp. 58, 57. The women in his early works are often left undeveloped, true, but they are never vilified.

11 Michael G. Lerner, *Pierre Loti* (New York, 1974), p. 5.

12 Raymonde Lefèvre, *Le Mariage de Loti* (Paris, 1935), p. 76. Jousselin's suggestions follow, pp. 77–91.

13 *Claude Monet: Biographie et catalogue raisonné*, ed. Daniel Wildenstein (Lausanne, 1974–91), letter 44.

14 Viaud told Daudet that he was inspired to do this by the reading of a book by Edmond de Goncourt that Daudet had given him (*Journal II* p. 167). Though Goncourt is largely forgotten now, and not without reason, he alone and with his brother Jules wrote several novels that were hailed in their day as successful transfers of Impressionism to literature. On this see Enzo Caramaschi, *Réalisme et impressionnisme dans l'oeuvre des frères Goncourt* (Pisa, n.d.). Recall the declaration by André Suarès quoted in the Introduction.

15 For a biography of Juliette Adam see *Et c'est moi, Juliette! Madame Adam 1836–1936* (Gif-sur-Yvette, 1988).

16 For the reviews see Lefèvre, *Mariage*, pp. 108–22.

17 Lefèvre, *Mariage*, p. 128.

18 On Gauguin's use of *The Marriage of Loti* in some of his early Tahitian paintings, see Richard M. Berrong, 'Oil Paintings of Word Paintings of Nature's Paintings: Gauguin's Early Tahitian Canvases and Pierre Loti's *Le Mariage de Loti (The Marriage of Loti)*, *Zeteo: The Journal of Interdisciplinary Writing* (Spring 2013): online at www.zeteojournal.com.

19 On what he has called Monet's 'personal legend' as a natural artist, see Paul Hayes Tucker, *Monet in the 90s* (Boston, MA, 1989), p. 27.

20 Monet had spent his time in the army in the early 1860s stationed in Algeria, perhaps because of his admiration for Eugène Delacroix, who had done some remarkable depictions of that country in the 1830s. After he finished his third novel Viaud informed another novelist friend, the now forgotten Émile Pouvillon, that he had tried to 'paint' regions of Africa in it (*Journal II*, p. 346), just as he recalled in his diary 'the great sad river [the Senegal?] that I tried to paint in *The Spahi*' (p. 357).

21 In fact, however, the last renters who occupied a part of the house would not leave until 19 October 1884 (*Journal II*, p. 557).

22 Raymonde Lefèvre, who was able to examine the manuscript, provides the first part of Jousselin's corrections/commentary in *En marge de Loti* (Paris, 1944), pp. 61–109.

23 There are two excellent books on Viaud's transformation of his house in Rochefort: Thierry Liot, *La Maison de Pierre Loti à Rochefort 1850–1923* (Chauray, 1999), and Alain Quella-Villéger, *Chez Pierre Loti: Une maison d'écrivain-voyageur* (Poitiers, 2008). Even if you don't read French, you will find the photos fascinating. For years after Viaud's son's death the house was maintained as a municipal museum. Unfortunately, structural problems became severe – Viaud did not imagine thousands of people trooping through his house when he transformed it.

24 *Journal I*, pp. 409, 418. Vercier and Quella-Villéger dismiss Viaud's claim as a 'fine lie' (*Journal II*, p. 328), and they seem to be right. When Le Cor was interviewed by journalist Paul Erio for *Le Journal* in 1926, three years after Viaud's death, he told the journalist that he had met the author for the first time in 1876 (*Le Journal*, 26 March 1876). In a letter to Juliette Adam from April 1880, Viaud assured his publisher that Le Cor was his childhood friend (*Adam*, p. 4).

25 *Journal I*, p. 416. The Druids, Celtic wise men and teachers, though they may have used megalithic monuments in their work, lived thousands of years after their erection by some still unknown people. Viaud, like most Frenchmen of his day, thought they had been contemporaneous.

26 *Pierre Loti dessinateur: Une oeuvre à long cours*, ed. Alain Quella-Villéger and Bruno Vercier (Saint-Pourçain-sur-Sioule, 2009), p. 228.

27 The most famous painter of the Gauls, the modern French name for the Celts who occupied Gaul during the time of Julius Caesar, was Évariste-Vital Luminais (1822–1896). Frédéric Auguste Bartholdi, who designed the Statue of Liberty, sculpted one of the most famous statues of Vercingétorix, which still stands in Clermont-Ferrand (see illustration in Chapter Four). Their Gauls are robust, hearty men who stood up to those so foolish as to invade Gaul/France – but they wore clothes.

28 With regard to Viaud's relationship with Pierre Le Cor, Blanch wrote: 'Loti was heterosexual, loving women passionately, and while he loved some men with equal fervour . . . it is clear that Pierre Le Cor

was, before all else, a *companion*', *Pierre Loti, the Legendary Romantic: A Biography* (New York, 1983), p. 128. If Viaud loved some men with a fervour equal to that he felt for women, how could he have been altogether heterosexual?

29 On Proust's extensive use of *My Brother Yves* see Richard M. Berrong, 'A Significant Source for the *Madeleine* and Other Major Episodes in *Combray*: Proust's Intertextual Use of Pierre Loti's *My Brother Yves*', *Studies in 20th & 21st Century Literature*, XXXVIII/1 (2014), Article 3, available at www.newprairiepress.org.

30 Valence and Pierre-Loti-Viaud, *La Famille*, p. 216.

31 The critical edition of *My Brother Yves* does not examine in detail how Viaud rearranged his diary to create the novel. To see that, in French, readers would have to consult my online edition of the work: www.personal.kent.edu/~rberrong/monfrereyves.

32 See *Journal II*, p. 352.

6 The Writer Becomes a Self-conscious Artist (1882–6)

1 Pierre Loti, *Fleurs d'ennui*, ed. Bruno Vercier (Paris, 2003), p. 21.

2 Pierre Loti, *Mon Frère Yves*, ed. Bruno Vercier (Paris, 1998), pp. 323–4.

3 Odette Valence and Samuel Pierre-Loti-Viaud, *La Famille de Pierre Loti; ou L'Éducation passionnée* (Paris, 1940), p. 218.

4 Loti, *Mon Frère Yves*, ed. Vercier, p. 326.

5 Ibid., pp. 323–4.

6 For these reviews see ibid., pp. 327–8.

7 See also ibid., p. 549.

8 There is now an immense literature on the beginning of the idea of distinct sexualities. Most of it grows out of the work of Michel Foucault, which has been called into question by historians.

9 For an overview of homosexuality in nineteenth-century French literature see Gretchen Schultz, 'French Literature: Nineteenth Century', in *The Gay and Lesbian Literary Heritage*, ed. Claude J. Summers (New York, 1995), pp. 293–8.

10 On this see Richard M. Berrong, 'A Significant Source for the *Madeleine* and Other Major Episodes in *Combray*: Proust's Intertextual Use of Pierre Loti's *My Brother Yves*', *Studies in 20th & 21st Century*

Literature, XXXVIII/1, Article 3, available at www.newprairiepress.org/sttcl/vol38/iss1/3.

11 Loti, *Mon Frère Yves*, ed. Vercier, p. 328.

12 Alain Quella-Villéger provides all the documents for what turned out to be a very complicated affair, *Pierre Loti: Le Pèlerin de la planète* (Bordeaux, 1998), pp. 95–105.

13 For a study of the role costumes played in Viaud's life see Peter James Turberfield, *Pierre Loti and the Theatricality of Desire* (Amsterdam, 2008).

14 On Japanese influences on Monet, see for example the exhibition catalogue *Monet and Japan* (Canberra, 2001).

15 Peter Brooks, *Henry James Goes to Paris* (Princeton, NJ, 2007), pp. 22, 59.

16 Raymonde Lefèvre, *En marge de Loti* (Paris, 1944), p. 51.

17 Henry James, 'Pierre Loti', in *Literary Criticism: French Writers, Other European Writers, the Prefaces to the New York Edition*, ed. Leon Edel (New York, 1984), p. 500.

18 For a study of this see Richard M. Berrong, 'Pierre Loti's Dialogue with *Germinal* and Naturalism: *Pêcheur d'Islande*', *Dalhousie French Studies*, 94 (2011), pp. 77–92.

19 Jan Walsh Hokenson, *Japan, France, and East–West Aesthetics: French Literature, 1867–2000* (Madison, NJ, 2004), p. 86.

20 On the sources and genesis of Puccini's opera, see Arthur Gross, 'Lieutenant F. B. Pinkerton: Problems in the Genesis and Performance of *Madama Butterfly*', *Italica*, LXIV/4 (1987), pp. 654–75.

21 John House, *Nature into Art* (New Haven, CT, 1988), p. 66.

22 On this see Richard M. Berrong, *Putting Monet and Rembrandt into Words* (Chapel Hill, NC, 2003), Ch. 1.

23 For a detailed study of these techniques, see ibid.

24 Guy de Maupassant, who followed his mentor Flaubert as a sort of extreme realist, condemned *Iceland Fisherman* in a review published in the 6 July 1886 edition of *Gil Blas*, a newspaper in which Zola serialized several of his own novels, for presenting an unrealistically positive portrayal of the Breton peasant, who, asserted Maupassant, 'was a sort of intermediary between man and beast'. There are no peasants in *Iceland Fisherman*. Pierre Loti, *Pêcheur d'Islande*, ed. Jacques Dupont (Paris, 1988), p. 318.

25 On this see Richard M. Berrong, 'Pierre Loti the Anti-colonialist: *Pêcheur d'Islande*', *Cincinnati Romance Review*, XXXIV (2012), pp. 34–46, available at www.cromrev.com.

26 On the homoerotic aspects of *Iceland Fisherman* see Richard M.
    Berrong, *In Love with a Handsome Sailor* (Toronto, 2003), Ch. 6.

27 Michael Moon, 'Disseminating Whitman', *Displacing Homophobia*,
    special issue of the *South Atlantic Quarterly*, ed. Ronald R. Butters, John
    M. Clum and Michael Moon, LXXXI/1 (1989), p. 260.

28 Quella-Villéger, *Pierre Loti: Le Pèlerin de la planète*, p. 120. Renan
    received Viaud in his home, Rosmapamon, outside Perros-Guirec,
    during a trip Viaud made to Paimpol to see the unnamed Paimpolaise
    just after *Iceland Fisherman* had finished its serialization in *La Nouvelle
    Revue* and appeared in book form.

7 Art, Memory and the Use of One to Highlight the Other
(1886–90)

 1 For a study of *Madame Chrysanthemum* as a critique of Zola's
    condemnation of Impressionism in *The Great Work of Art*, see Richard
    M. Berrong, *Putting Monet and Rembrandt into Words* (Chapel Hill, NC,
    2013), Ch. 2.

 2 The great Zola scholar Henri Mitterand provides Goncourt's
    disdainful comments on *The Great Work of Art* in the rich
    documentation for his critical edition of *L'Oeuvre* (Paris, 1983), pp.
    444–5. Goncourt saw Zola's latest novel as an inferior reworking of
    Manette Salomon, a fiction about artists that Goncourt had written
    twenty years before with his late brother Jules. *The Great Work of Art* is
    not without its faults, but it is still superior to the Goncourt tome, at
    least in my opinion.

 3 For the complications this edition caused Viaud – he had forgotten
    that he was still under contract to Calmann-Lévy – see the introduction
    to *Madame Chrysanthème*, ed. Bruno Vercier (Paris, 1990), pp. 38–9. On
    the pricing of the original editions of Viaud's novels, see Hector Talvart
    and Joseph Place, *Bibliographie des auteurs modernes de langue française
    (1801–1953)* (Paris, 1954), vol. XII, pp. 255–76.

 4 On what came to be known as the 'Impressionist frame' see Anthea
    Callen, *The Art of Impressionism* (New Haven, CT, 2008), p. 194.

 5 For an analysis of this scene see Berrong, *Putting Monet and Rembrandt
    into Words*, Ch. 2.

6 Vincent van Gogh, *Lettres de Vincent van Gogh à son frère Théo*, ed. Georges Philippart (Paris, 1937), p. 206.

7 The most nuanced and intelligent study of this issue, at least in my eyes, is to be found in Ch. 1 of Akane Kawakami, *Travellers' Visions: French Literary Encounters with Japan, 1881–2004* (Liverpool, 2005).

8 Even the first English translation brought out by Frederick A. Stokes preserved the wide margins, spacing and Rossi and Myrbach illustrations.

9 'Eugène Delacroix: The Complete Works'/'Biography of Eugène Delacroix', www.eugenedelacroix.org/biography.html, accessed 13 December 2017.

10 Pierre Loti, *Au Maroc*, in the 21 September 1889 instalment of *L'Illustration*, p. 241.

11 This lavish edition, too, was published in English with all the illustrations – though the large magazine page size was not retained by New York publisher Welch, Fracker Company – at the end of 1889.

12 The Sigmaringen castle would serve as the refuge of Philippe Pétain and his Vichy government when the Germans 'rescued' them from the Allied forces that landed in France in 1944. Viaud would have an encounter with Pétain during the First World War, as recounted in Chapter Eleven.

13 For all the details behind this see Alain Quella-Villéger, 'L'Exote et l'exilée: Une amitié littéraire originale', in *Avec l'exilée à Sinaia, Bucarest, Venise*, ed. Alain Quella-Villéger (Mignaloux-Beauvoir, 2016), pp. 16–24.

14 For the correspondence between Viaud and the Queen see *Avec l'exilée*, pp. 189–233.

15 Ibid., p. 220.

16 For a study of *The Story of a Child* from this perspective, see Berrong, *Putting Monet and Rembrandt into Words*, Ch. 3.

17 See Marcel Proust, *Correspondence*, ed. Philip Kolb, vol. I (Paris, 1970), p. 138.

18 On this and other costume parties that Viaud staged in his home, see Alain Quella-Villéger, *Chez Pierre Loti: Une maison d'écrivain-voyageur* (Poitiers, 2008).

19 Alain Quella-Villéger, *Pierre Loti: Le Pèlerin de la planète* (Bordeaux, 1998), p. 125.

20 Sacha Guitry, *La Maison de Loti* (Paris, 1931).

21 Pierre Loti, *Matelot*, ed. Bruno Vercier (Paris, 2004), p. 200.

8 Life at the Top (1891–1900)

1 On the construction of these rooms, including the mosque, see Thierry Liot, *La Maison de Pierre Loti à Rochefort 1850–1923* (Chauray, 1999), pp. 59–66. Even if you can't read the French text, you can marvel at the colour photographs of the rooms. There is also a good, picture-filled website, again only in French, at www.maisondepierreloti.fr with information about the restoration.

2 On this first election attempt see Alain Quella-Villéger, *Pierre Loti: Le Pèlerin de la planète* (Bordeaux, 1998), pp. 194–5. Also *Journal III*, p. 316.

3 On the politics behind Viaud's election to the French Academy, see Quella-Villéger, *Le Pèlerin de la planète*, pp. 195–8.

4 Mary Dailey Desmarais, 'Hunting for Light: *Luncheon on the Grass*', in *Monet: The Early Years*, ed. George T. M. Shackelford (New Haven, CT, 2016), pp. 20–33.

5 For some of the press reaction to Viaud's election, see Quella-Villéger, *Le Pèlerin de la planète*, pp. 195–6.

6 For these texts see Quella-Villéger, *Le Pèlerin de la planète*, pp. 200–201.

7 Gaston Mauberger, *Dans l'intimité de Pierre Loti (1903–1923)*, ed. Alain Quella-Villéger (Saintes, 2003), p. 335.

8 For the passages in Goncourt's diary see Quella-Villéger, *Le Pèlerin de la planète*, pp. 198–9.

9 On Geneviève Straus' salon, see William C. Carter, *Marcel Proust: A Life* (New Haven, CT, 2000), pp. 90–95.

10 Henry James, 'Pierre Loti', in *Literary Criticism: French Writers, Other European Writers, the Prefaces to the New York Edition*, ed. Leon Edel (New York, 1984), p. 518. This passage comes from James's preface to the translation of a collection of short Viaud pieces entitled, in English, *Impressions*.

11 Alain Quella-Villéger, 'L'Exote et l'exilée: Une amitié littéraire originale', in *Avec l'exilée à Sinaia, Bucarest, Venise*, ed. Alain Quella-Villéger (Mignaloux-Beauvoir, 2016), p. 76; on the relationship between Juliette Adam and Viaud during this period, see pp. 76–9.

12 André Antoine, 'Lettre', *Mercure de Flandre*, 10 (January–February 1931), p. 34.

13 Pierre Loti, *Judith Renaudin*, *La Revue de Paris*, 5 (1898), pp. 2–3. When the play was reprinted in book form, the final paragraphs of the 'Avant-propos' (preface), including this passage, were cut (see Pierre Loti, *Judith Renaudin* [Paris, 1898], p. iii). The book edition was reprinted through the years without alteration. Those final paragraphs, including the passage in question, are also absent from the edition of the play found in the tome devoted to Viaud's theatre that was published by Calmann-Lévy in 1911 as part of his *Oeuvres complètes* (Pierre Loti, *Oeuvres completes* [Paris, 1911], vol. II, p. iii).

14 But this, too, may have been a white lie. Guy Dugas and Claude Duvigneau, in their introduction to an edition of the play, show how, with those words, Viaud was trying to assure his readers that the play was not a commentary on the Dreyfus Affair, which by 1898 was raging in Paris ('La Fibre protestante', in *Pierre Loti et son pays natal* [Paris, 1998], p. 139). While I do not see that Viaud wrote the play to comment on that political upheaval, he may well have lied about when he first started work on it in order to forestall any accusations to the contrary.

15 Robert Gottlieb, *Sarah: The Life of Sarah Bernhardt* (New Haven, CT, 2010), p. 146. The most detailed study of the actress and her repertory is Ernest Pronier's *Sarah Bernhardt* (Geneva, n.d.).

16 *Journal IV*, p. 225. In 1899 Viaud was working on another play, *Yvonne Lescure*, of which only the first and third acts survive. A contemporary story dealing with two artists overpowered by desire for much younger individuals that could lead to their public humiliation, it reads as if it was tailor-made for Bernhardt – and perhaps a reflection of Viaud's worries about his relationship with Léo Thémèze. In his preface to the play published in the bulletin of the *Association internationale des amis de Pierre Loti*, 2nd series, 5 (1951), pp. 8–9, the editor, Fernand Laplaud, speculated that this was the play that Viaud was talking about in his 1895–6 diary entries, but the reference to the Edict of Nantes, which Laplaud does not seem to have been aware of, makes that impossible.

17 On the reaction in the French press to the Wilde trials, see Nancy Erber, 'The French Trials of Oscar Wilde', *Journal of the History of Sexuality*, VI/4 (1996), pp. 549–88. Wilde had sent Viaud an autographed copy of *Salomé* in 1893 (Quella-Villéger, *Le Pèlerin de la*

planète, p. 212), for which Viaud wrote the Irish poet a flattering thank-you note (Richard Ellmann, *Oscar Wilde* [New York, 1988], p. 375).

18 J. E. Rivers, *Proust and the Art of Love* (New York, 1980), p. 110.

19 Quoted in Quella-Villéger, 'L'Exote et l'exilée', p. 78.

20 Quoted ibid., pp. 79–80.

21 On this interpretation of *Judith Renaudin*, see Richard M. Berrong, 'A French Reaction to the Wilde Affair and Increasing Homophobia in Late-Nineteenth-century France: Pierre Loti's *Judith Renaudin*', *Neophilologus*, xcv/2 (2011), pp. 177–89.

22 Mauberger, *Dans l'intimité*, p. 292.

23 Pierre Loti, *Matelot*, ed. Bruno Vercier (Paris, 2004), p. 210.

24 Loti, *A Pilgrimage to Angkor*, Ch. 13. David McKay's English translation of this work has been published as *A Pilgrimage to Angkor* and *Siam*, the latter a strange title, since Angkor Wat is located in Cambodia and not Siam.

25 The source for this part of the novel is a description of Joseph Brahy during a trip inland to learn about his birthplace: *Journal III*, p. 507.

26 On Conrad's use of *Ramuntcho* in 'Heart of Darkness' see: Richard M. Berrong, '"Heart of Darkness" and Pierre Loti's *Ramuntcho*: Fulcrum for a Masterpiece', *The Conradian*, xxxv/1 (Spring 2010), pp. 28–44.

27 Alison McQueen, *The Rise of the Cult of Rembrandt: Reinventing an Old Master in Nineteenth-century France* (Amsterdam, 2003), p. 16.

28 Ibid., p. 109.

29 Ibid., p. 119.

30 Jean Joseph-Renaud, 'J'ai connu Pierre Loti', clipped from a newspaper without name or date.

31 For a detailed explanation of this interpretation of *Ramuntcho*, see Richard M. Berrong, *Putting Monet and Rembrandt into Words* (Chapel Hill, NC, 2013), Ch. 4.

32 For Viaud's photographs taken in India and Persia see: *Les Orients de Pierre Loti*, ed. Bruno Vercier (Paris, 2006) and *Pierre Loti photographe*, ed. Alain Quella-Villéger and Bruno Vercier (Saint-Pourçain-sur-Sioule, 2012).

9 A Feminist in Spite of Himself? (1900–1906)

1 Jean Joseph-Renaud, 'J'ai connu Pierre Loti'. This article was published in some French newspaper, but since I have only the clipping I do not know the date it appeared or even the name of the newspaper. On the same page there is a mention of 'Jules Romans of the French Academy'. Romans was not elected to that body until 1946, so the article cannot date from earlier than that. Joseph-Renaud died in 1953, so that is probably the *terminus post quam*.

2 John House, *Nature into Art* (New Haven, CT, 1986), p. 224.

3 Ibid., p. 22. See also Robert L. Herbert, 'Method and Meaning in Monet', *Art in America*, LVII (September 1979), pp. 80–108, on the work Monet put into making his canvases appear spontaneous even when they were the result of a lot of careful study.

4 House, *Nature into Art*, p. 165.

5 On this see for example Ross King, *Mad Enchantment: Claude Monet and the Painting of the Water Lilies* (New York, 2016), Ch. 3.

6 On the painterly artistry of the travel narratives see Richard M. Berrong, *Putting Monet and Rembrandt into Words* (Chapel Hill, NC, 2013), Ch. 3.

7 Photography can be an art as well. No one knew that better than Viaud, who was very interested in it and took sometimes fascinating photographs around the world. The photographs used in the *Illustration* pages are not artistic, however.

8 On the writing of *The Daughter of Heaven* see Michael G. Lerner, *Pierre Loti's Dramatic Works* (Lewiston, NY, 1998), Ch. 4.

9 Gaston Mauberger, *Dans l'intimité de Pierre Loti (1903–1923)*, ed. Alain Quella-Villéger (Saintes, 2003), pp. 23–4.

10 Pierre Loti, 'New York entrevu par un Oriental très vieux jeu', *The Century* (February–March 1913). It was reprinted in a 1917 collection of Viaud's essays entitled *Quelques aspects du vertige mondial*, which has not been translated into English.

11 On the production, reviews and so on, see Richard M. Berrong, '*La Fille du ciel* à New York', *Bulletin de l'Association pour la Maison Pierre Loti*, 24 (2012), pp. 14–19; and Lerner, *Pierre Loti's Dramatic Works*, Ch. 4.

12 Pierre Loti, *Matelot*, ed. Bruno Vercier (Paris, 2004), p. 212.

13 *Les Désenchantées* has been published in Clara Bell's English translation

as *The Disenchanted*, though the text makes clear that the title should be something like *The Awakened*, since the main character uses the word to describe modern Turkish women who have thrown off the blinding enchantment of tradition to see their rights and the place they deserve in modern Turkish society.

14 Bruno Vercier and Alain Quella-Villéger, 'Un étrange roman', in Pierre Loti, *Les Désenchantées* (Aicirits, 2003), p. 11.

15 After spending most of her monograph excoriating Viaud for being a woman-denigrating homosexual, Irene L. Szyliowicz declares that '*Les Désenchantées* . . . represents a milestone in feminist thought for the early twentieth century because it pleads for equal rights for women at a time when they were mostly regarded as second-class citizens', *Pierre Loti and the Oriental Woman* (New York, 1988), p. 94.

16 For the story of these two women see Alain Quella-Villéger, *Evadées du harem: Affaire d'Etat et féminisme à Constantinople (1906)* (Paris, 2015).

17 Pierre Loti, *Suprêmes visions d'Orient* (Paris, 1921), Ch. 13. The actual diary entry itself, only two short paragraphs and not five pages as in *Supreme Visions of the East*, makes no mention of an investigation into the last days of Leyla (*Journal v*, p. 483).

18 See the preface to and first chapter of Marc Hélys, *Le Secret des 'Désenchantées'* (Paris, 1924).

19 Hélys, *Le Secret des 'Désenchantées'*, Preface.

20 On this interpretation of the novel see Richard M. Berrong, *In Love with a Handsome Sailor* (Toronto, 2003), Ch. 11.

10 Loti the Turkophile (1907–14)

1 Schlumberger's article appeared in the June 1913 issue of *La Nouvelle Revue française*. Claude Martin quotes the passage in question in his introduction to the text, in Loti, *Voyages (1872–1913)*, ed. Claude Martin (Paris, 1991), p. 1241.

2 Martin, 'Introduction', in Pierre Loti, *Voyages (1872–1913)*, p. 1241.

3 Gaston Mauberger, *Dans l'intimité de Pierre Loti (1903–1923)*, ed. Alain Quella-Villéger (Saintes, 2003), p. 94.

4 Ibid., p. 125.

5 Ibid., p. 107.
6 Ibid., p. 69.
7 For Mauberger's article and a description of the evening see ibid, pp. 112–13.

11 Diplomat and War Correspondent (1914–18)

1 Gaston Mauberger, *Dans l'intimité de Pierre Loti (1903–1923)*, ed. Alain Quella-Villéger (Saintes, 2003), p. 212.
2 Pierre Loti, 'La Basilique-fantôme', in *La Hyène enragée* (Paris, 1916), p. 48.
3 Ibid., p. 50.
4 Ibid., p. 51.
5 Ibid., p. 56.
6 For a study of Viaud's article on Reims Cathedral see Richard M. Berrong, 'Tableau de cathédrale = tableau de la nation et du peuple français: Pierre Loti, Victor Hugo, et Claude Monet: La Basilique fantôme de Reims', *Le Bulletin de l'Association internationale des amis de Pierre Loti*, 32 (June 2015), pp. 2–10.
7 In 1917 two officials of the French government asked Monet, who had symbolized the greatness of the nation in his *Rouen Cathedral* series two decades before, to convey the significance of the destruction of Reims Cathedral in a painting. For this story see Ross King, *Mad Enchantment: Claude Monet and the Painting of the Water Lilies* (New York, 1916), Chs 9–10.

12 Last Years (1919–23)

1 Gaston Mauberger, *Dans l'intimité de Pierre Loti (1903–1923)*, ed. Alain Quella-Villéger (Santes, 2003), p. 353. For the correspondence between Atatürk and Viaud see *Pierre Loti: Lettres pour la Turquie* (Ankara, 2000).
2 Mauberger, *Dans l'intimité de Pierre Loti*, pp. 321, 327.
3 Ibid., p. 330.

4   Ibid., p. 335.
5   Ibid., p. 388.
6   Ibid., p. 391.
7   The silent newsreel coverage of the ceremony is on the DVD that accompanies Alain Quella-Villéger, *Chez Pierre Loti: Une maison d'écrivain-voyageur* (n.p., 2008).

Select Bibliography

Published volumes by Pierre Loti

Most of Pierre Loti's works appeared in English (as well as many other languages) within a few years of their initial French publication. These translations can often be found in larger public libraries. There are also inexpensive modern reprints of them available on the Internet, since they are no longer subject to copyright. His better-known works continue to appear in modern editions in France: the novels often in Gallimard's Folio collection or the GF collection from Flammarion; the travel narrations and other works with other publishers. A bibliography of everything Viaud published, including all the newspaper articles, prefaces, and so on, can be found in the appendices of the critical edition of Viaud's diary (see below). Below is a chronological list of the volumes he published, with an indication of their genre – a difficult distinction in many cases. For those that have been translated into English, I give the various titles under which they have appeared in italics.

Aziyadé (1879), novel; *Aziyadé*; *Constantinople*
Le Mariage de Loti (1880), novel; *The Marriage of Loti*; *Rarahu*; *Tahiti*
Le Roman d'un spahi (1881), novel; *Between Two Opinions*; *Love in the Desert*;
    The Romance of a Spahi; *The Sahara*; *A Spahi's Love-story*
Fleurs d'ennui (1882), collection of pieces; no English translation
Mon Frère Yves (1883), novel; *My Brother Yves*; *A Tale of Brittany*
Pêcheur d'Islande (1886), novel; *Iceland Fisherman*
Propos d'exil (1887), collection of pieces; *From Lands of Exile*
Madame Chrysanthème (1887), novel; *Madame Chrysanthemum*; *Japan*
Japoneries d'automne (1889), collection of pieces; no English translation in
    volume form
Au Maroc (1890), travel narrative; *Morocco*; *Into Morocco*

Le Roman d'un enfant (1890), novel; *A Child's Romance*; *The Romance of a Child*; *The Story of a Child*

Le Livre de la pitié et de la mort (1891), collection of pieces; *The Book of Pity and of Death*

Fantôme d'Orient (1891), novel; *A Phantom from the East*

Discours de réception à l'Académie française (1892), speech; no English translation

L'Exilée (1893), collection of pieces; *Carmen Sylva and Sketches from the Orient*

Matelot (1893), novel; *Jean Berny, Sailor*

Pêcheur d'Islande (1893), drama; no English translation

Le Désert (1895), travel narrative; *The Desert*

Jérusalem (1895), travel narrative; *Jerusalem*

Galilée (1895), travel narrative; no English translation

Ramuntcho (1897), novel; *Ramuntcho*; *A Tale of the Pyrenees*

Figures et choses qui passaient (1897), collection of pieces; *Impressions*

Judith Renaudin (1898), drama; no English translation

Reflets sur la sombre route (1899), collection of pieces; *On Life's Byways*

Les Derniers Jours de Pékin (1902), travel narrative; *The Last Days of Peking*

L'Inde (sans les Anglais) (1903), travel narrative; *India*

Vers Ispahan (1904), travel narrative; no English translation

La Troisième Jeunesse de Madame Prune (1905), novel; *Madame Prune*

Les Désenchantées (1906), novel; *The Disenchanted*

Ramuntcho (1908), drama; no English translation

La Mort de Philae (1909), travel narrative; *Egypt*

Le Château de la Belle au bois dormant (1910), collection of pieces; no English translation

La Fille du ciel (1911), drama written with Judith Gautier; *The Daughter of Heaven*

Un Pèlerin d'Angkor (1912), travel narrative; *A Pilgrimage to Angkor*; *Siam*

Turquie agonisante (1913), collection of pieces; *Turkey in Agony*

La Hyène enragée (1916), collection of pieces; *War*

Quelques aspects du vertige mondial (1917), collection of pieces; no English translation

L'Horreur allemande (1918), collection of pieces; no English translation

Prime Jeunesse (1919), novel/autobiography; no English translation

Suprêmes Visions d'Orient (1921), travel narrative; no English translation

Viaud's Correspondence

Correspondance inédite 1865–1904, ed. Nadine Duvignau and N. Serban
   (Paris, 1929)
Lettres de Pierre Loti à Madame Juliette Adam (1880–1922) (Paris, 1924)
'Les Deux chattes sont à leur poste, et les décors s'achèvent . . .', ed. Guy
   Dugas (Alluyes, 2000)
Valence, Odette, and Samuel Pierre-Loti-Viaud, *La Famille de Pierre Loti;
   ou, L'Éducation passionnée* (Paris, 1940)
Pierre Loti: Lettres pour la Turquie (Ankara, 2000)
Shorter collections of letters are indicated in the endnotes.

Viaud's Diary

The critical edition of Viaud's diary, edited by Alain Quella-Villéger and
Bruno Vercier, consists of five volumes entitled *Journal* containing the
diary from 1868 until 1913 and one volume entitled *Soldats bleus* containing
the diary from the war years, 1914–18. It supersedes all previous partial
editions, including those published by Viaud's son at the end of Viaud's life.

Viaud's Art

Pierre Loti dessinateur: Une oeuvre au long cours, ed. Alain Quella-Villéger and
   Bruno Vercier (Saint-Pourçain-sur-Sioule, 2009)

Biographical Works on Loti

The only scholarly biography of Viaud is Alain Quella-Villéger's *Pierre Loti:
Le Pèlerin de la planète* (Bordeaux, 1998), which has not been translated
into English. English-language popular biographies, including Lesley
Blanch's *Pierre Loti, The Legendary Romantic* (New York, 1983), rely too
much on Viaud's fiction and not enough on historical documentation.
They mix the real Julien Viaud with the personas he spent much of his life
developing for public consumption.

Also useful are the introductions and notes to the French critical editions of Viaud's works published by Bruno Vercier, Alain Quella-Villéger and Claude Martin. These are cited in the endnotes.

Works about Loti and His Writing

Antoine, André, 'Lettre', *Mercure de Flandre*, 10 (January–February 1931), pp. 34–8

Barthes, Roland, 'Pierre Loti: *Aziyadé*', in *New Critical Essays*, trans. Richard Howard (New York, 1980), pp. 105–121

Berrong, Richard M., 'Les Editions illustrées des romans de Pierre Loti', *Le Bulletin de l'Association internationale des amis de Pierre Loti*, 15 (2006), pp. 2–13, and 'Addendum', 16 (2007), pp. 6–8

—, '*La Fille du ciel* à New York', *Bulletin de l'Association pour la Maison Pierre Loti*, 24 (2012), pp. 14–19

—, 'A French Reaction to the Wilde Affair and Increasing Homophobia in Late-nineteenth-century France: Pierre Loti's *Judith Renaudin*', *Neophilologus*, xcv/2 (2011), pp. 177–89

—, '"Heart of Darkness" and Pierre Loti's *Ramuntcho*: Fulcrum for a Masterpiece', *The Conradian*, xxxv/1 (Spring 2010), pp. 28–44

—, *In Love with a Handsome Sailor* (Toronto, 2003)

—, 'Oil Paintings of Word Paintings of Nature's Paintings: Gauguin's Early Tahitian Canvases and Pierre Loti's *Le Mariage de Loti* (*The Marriage of Loti*)', *Zeteo: The Journal of Interdisciplinary Writing* (Spring 2013), www.zeteojournal.com

—, 'Pierre Loti the Anti-colonialist: *Pêcheur d'Islande*', *Cincinnati Romance Review*, 34 (2012), pp. 34–46

—, 'Pierre Loti's Dialogue with *Germinal* and Naturalism: *Pêcheur d'Islande*', *Dalhousie French Studies*, 94 (2011), pp. 77–92

—, *Putting Monet and Rembrandt into Words* (Chapel Hill, nc, 2003)

—, 'A Significant Source for the *Madeleine* and Other Major Episodes in *Combray*: Proust's Intertextual Use of Pierre Loti's *My Brother Yves*', *Studies in 20th & 21st Century Literature*, xxxviii/1, Article 3, www.newprairiepress.org

—, 'Tableau de cathédrale = tableau de la nation et du peuple français: Pierre Loti, Victor Hugo, et Claude Monet: La Basilique fantôme de

Reims', *Le Bulletin de l'Association internationale des amis de Pierre Loti*, 32 (June 2015), pp. 2–10

Blanch, Lesley, *Pierre Loti, the Legendary Romantic: A Biography* (New York, 1983)

Bongie, Chris, *Exotic Memories: Literature, Colonialism, and the Fin de Siècle* (Stanford, CA, 1991)

Buisine, Alain, *Tombeau de Loti* (Paris, 1988)

Combelles, Pierre-Oliver, *L'Île de Pâques: Journal d'un aspirant de La Flore* (Ville-d'Avray, 1988)

Dugas, Guy, and Claude Duvigneau, 'La Fibre protestante', in *Pierre Loti et son pays natal*, ed. Claude Duvigneau (Paris, 1998), pp. 133–9

Ferrand, Frank, 'Rochefort: Pierre Loti's Planet', *France Today* (March 2007), p. 17

Genet, Christian, and Daniel Hervé, *Pierre Loti l'enchanteur* (Gemozac, 1988)

Grenouilleau, Anne-Dominique, 'Le Nom de Loti et le vocabulaire tahitien dans *Le Mariage de Loti*', *Revue Pierre Loti*, 7 (July–September 1981)

Gross, Arthur, 'Lieutenant F. B. Pinkerton: Problems in the Genesis and Performance of *Madama Butterfly*', *Italica*, LXIV/4 (1987), pp. 654–75

Guitry, Sacha, *La Maison de Loti* (Paris, 1931)

Hargreaves, Alec G., *The Colonial Experience in French Fiction* (London, 1981)

Hélys, Marc, *Le Secret des 'Désenchantées'* (Paris, 1924)

James, Henry, 'Pierre Loti', in *Literary Criticism: French Writers, Other European Writers, The Prefaces to the New York Edition*, ed. Leon Edel (New York, 1984)

Kawakami, Akane, *Travellers' Visions: French Literary Encounters with Japan, 1881–2004* (Liverpool, 2005)

Lefèvre, Raymonde, *Les Désenchantées de Pierre Loti* (Paris, 1939)

—, *En marge de Loti* (Paris, 1944)

—, *Le Mariage de Loti* (Paris, 1935)

Lerner, Michael G., *Pierre Loti* (New York, 1974)

—, *Pierre Loti's Dramatic Works* (Lewiston, NY, 1998)

Liot, Thierry, *La Maison de Pierre Loti à Rochefort 1850–1923* (Chauray, 1999)

Loti, Pierre, *Les Orients de Pierre Loti*, ed. Bruno Vercier (Paris, 2006)

—, *Pierre Loti photographe*, ed. Alain Quella-Villéger, Bruno Vercier (Saint-Pourçain-sur-Sioule, 2012)

Matsuda, Matt K., *Empire of Love: Histories of France and the Pacific* (New York, 2005)

Mauberger, Gaston, *Dans l'intimité de Pierre Loti (1903–1923)*, ed. Alain Quella-Villéger (Saintes, 2003)

Melchiori, Barbara, 'Feelings about Aspects: Henry James on Pierre Loti', *Studi americani*, 15 (1969), pp. 169–99

Millward, Keith G., *L'Oeuvre de Pierre Loti et l'esprit 'fin de siècle'* (Paris, 1955)

Moon, Michael, 'Disseminating Whitman', *Displacing Homophobia*, special issue of the *South Atlantic Quarterly*, ed. Ronald R. Butters, John M. Clum and Michael Moon, LXXXVIII/1 (1989), pp. 247–65

Morin, Jeanne Elise, 'De "Au large" à "Pêcheur d'Islande"', *Revue Pierre Loti*, 27 (1986), p. 49.

Moulis, André, 'Genèse de "Ramuntcho"', *Littératures*, 12 (1965), pp. 49–78

Ono, Setsuko, *A Western Image of Japan* (Geneva, 1972)

Osaji, Debe, 'The African Image by a Non-African Novelist Dealing with Africa: A Case-study of *Le Roman d'un Spahi* by Pierre Loti', *Nigeria Magazine*, LIV/3 (1986), pp. 97–103

Proust, Marcel, *Correspondence*, ed. Philip Kolb, vol. I (Paris, 1970)

Quella-Villéger, Alain, *Chez Pierre Loti: Une maison d'écrivain-voyageur* (n.p., 2008)

—, *Evadées du harem: Affaire d'etat et féminisme à Constantinople (1906)* (Paris, 2015)

—, 'L'Exote et l'exilée: Une amitié littéraire originale', in *Avec l'exilée à Sinaia, Bucarest, Venise*, ed. Alain Quella-Villéger (Mignaloux-Beauvoir, 2016)

—, *Pierre Loti: Le Pèlerin de la planète* (Bordeaux, 1998)

Saint-Léger, Marie-Paule de, *Pierre Loti l'insaisissable* (Paris, 1996)

Scepi, Henri, 'Rhétorique de l'incertain dans *Pêcheur d'Islande*', *Revue Pierre Loti*, 27 (1986), pp. 65–8

Sharpley-Whiting, T. Denean, *Sexualized Savages, Primal Fears, and Primitive Narratives in French* (Durham, NC, 1999)

Suarès, André, 'Loti', *Présences* (Paris, 1926)

Szyliowicz, Irene L., *Pierre Loti and the Oriental Woman* (New York, 1962)

Turberfield, Peter James, *Pierre Loti and the Theatricality of Desire* (Amsterdam, 2008)

Valence, Odette, and Samuel Pierre-Loti-Viaud, *La Famille de Pierre Loti; ou L'Éducation passionnée* (Paris, 1940)

Van Gogh, Vincent, *Lettres de Vincent van Gogh à son frère Théo*, ed. Georges Philippart (Paris, 1937)

Wake, Clive, *The Novels of Pierre Loti* (The Hague, 1974)

Works on Viaud's Era, and the Context of His Life and Works

Bohlke, L. Brent, and Sharon Hoover, eds, *Willa Cather Remembered* (Lincoln, NE, 2002)

Brooks, Peter, *Henry James Goes to Paris* (Princeton, NJ, 2007)

Callen, Anthea, *The Art of Impressionism* (New Haven, CT, 2008)

Caramaschi, Enzo, *Réalisme et impressionnisme dans l'oeuvre des frères Goncourt* (Pisa, n.d.)

Carter, William C., *Marcel Proust: A Life* (New Haven, CT, 2000)

Chernowitz, Maurice E., *Proust and Painting* (New York, 1945)

Copley, Antony, *Sexual Moralities in France, 1790–1980: New Ideas on the Family, Divorce, and Homosexuality* (London, 1989)

Desbonnet, Edmond, *Comment on devient athlète* (Paris, 1937)

Desmarais, Mary Dailey, 'Hunting for Light: *Luncheon on the Grass*', in *Monet: The Early Years*, ed. George T. M. Shackelford (New Haven, CT, 2016), pp. 20–33

Ellmann, Richard, *Oscar Wilde* (New York, 1988)

Erber, Nancy, 'The French Trials of Oscar Wilde', *Journal of the History of Sexuality*, VI/4 (1996), pp. 549–88

Et c'est moi, Juliette! Madame Adam 1836–1936 (Gif-sur-Yvette, 1988)

Foucault, Michel, *History of Sexuality*, vol. I, trans. Robert Hurley (New York, 1990)

Gottlieb, Robert, *Sarah: The Life of Sarah Bernhardt* (New Haven, CT, 2010)

Halperin, David M., 'How to Do the History of Male Homosexuality', *GLQ: A Journal of Lesbian and Gay Studies*, VI/1 (2000), pp. 87–123

Herbert, Robert L., 'Method and Meaning in Monet', *Art in America*, 67 (1979), pp. 80–108

Hokenson, Jan Walsh, *Japan, France, and East–West Aesthetics: French Literature, 1867–2000* (Madison, NJ, 2004)

House, John, *Nature into Art* (New Haven, CT, 1988)

King, Ross, *The Judgment of Paris* (New York, 2006)

—, *Mad Enchantment: Claude Monet and the Painting of the Water Lilies* (New York, 2016)

McQueen, Alison, *The Rise of the Cult of Rembrandt: Reinventing an Old Master in Nineteenth-century France* (Amsterdam, 2003)

Martin, Paul M., *Vercingétorix: Le Politique, le stratège* (Paris, 2000)

Monet and Japan, exh.cat., National Gallery of Australia, Canberra (2001)

Muhlstein, Anka, 'Painters and Writers: When Something New Happens',
    New York Review of Books, LXIV/1 (2017), pp. 33–5
Nye, Robert A., *Masculinity and Male Codes of Honor in Modern France*
    (Berkeley, CA, 1993)
Pomian, Krzysztof, 'Francs et Gaulois', in *Les Lieux de mémoire*, ed. Pierre
    Nora (Paris, 1992), vol. III, pp. 41–105
Proust, Marcel, *Correspondence*, ed. Philip Kolb, vol. I (Paris, 1970)
Rivers, J. E., *Proust and the Art of Love* (New York, 1980)
Rosario, Vernon A., 'Inversion's Histories / History's Inversions: Novelizing
    Fin-de-siècle Homosexuality', in *Science and Homosexualities*, ed.
    Vernon A. Rosario (New York, 1997), pp. 89–107
—, 'Pointy Penises, Fashion Crimes, and Hysterical Mollies: The Pederasts'
    Inversions', in *Homosexuality in Modern France*, ed. Jeffrey Merrick and
    Bryant T. Ragan Jr (New York, 1996), pp. 146–76
Said, Edward, *Orientalism* (New York, 1979)
Schultz, Gretchen, 'French Literature: Nineteenth Century', in *The Gay and
    Lesbian Literary Heritage*, ed. Claude J. Summers (New York, 1995), pp. 293–8
Sedgwick, Eve Kosofsky, *Epistemology of the Closet* (Berkeley, CA, 1990)
Tucker, Paul Hayes, *Monet in the 90s* (Boston, MA, 1989)
Turner, William B., *A Genealogy of Queer Theory* (Philadelphia, PA, 2000)
Waldrep, Shelton, *The Aesthetics of Self-invention: Oscar Wilde to David Bowie*
    (Minneapolis, MN, 2004)
Wildenstein, Daniel, *Claude Monet: Biographie et catalogue raisonné*, 5 vols
    (Lausanne, 1974–91)
Woodress, James, *Willa Cather: A Literary Life* (Lincoln, NE, 1987)

Acknowledgements

I have been working on Pierre Loti for almost twenty years now. Throughout that time the two great Loti scholars, Bruno Vercier and Alain Quella-Villéger, have answered many an email. I thank them here for all the information they provided me as I wrote this book.

I would also like to thank Kent State University for the sabbatical that allowed me to pull much of this book together, after years of working on it.

Photo Acknowledgements

The author and publishers wish to express their thanks to the below sources of illustrative material and/or permission to reproduce it. Some locations of artworks are also given below, in the interests of brevity:

Richard Berrong: pp. 70, 101, 173; Bibliothèque nationale de France: pp. 150, 177; from *L'Illustration*: pp. 41 (1872), 107 (1889); from Paul Iribe, *L'Assiette au beurre*, vol. CIX (1903): p. 82; Library of Congress, Washington, DC: p. 110; Musée des Augustins, Toulouse: p. 106; Musée de Louvre: pp. 28, 29; from Pierre Loti, *Journal*, vol. III (Paris, 2012): p. 143; from Pierre Loti, *The Daughter of Heaven* (New York, 1912): p. 157; Musée du Luxembourg, Paris: p. 105; Metropolitan Museum of Art, New York: p. 178; Rijksmuseum, Amsterdam: pp. 27; Rochefort Municipal Museums: pp. 15, 16, 17, 38, 44, 66, 69, 86, 115, 117, 120, 123 (photo V. Lagardère), 127, 158, 159; Jacques Viaud: p. 37.